Sushi for Wimps

Sushi for Wimps

Seaweed to Dragon Rolls
for the Faint of Heart

Aya Imatani

Photography by Matt Cohen

Sterling Publishing Co., Inc.
New York

Created by Penn Publishing Ltd.
Design by Michel Opatowski
Photography by Matt Cohen
Editor: Phyllis Glazer

10 9 8 7 6 5 4 3 2

Library of Congress Cataloging-in-Publication Data

Imatani, Aya.
   Sushi for wimps: seaweed to dragon rolls for the faint of heart/Aya Imatani;
photography by Matt Cohen.
      p. cm.
   Includes index.
   ISBN 1-4027-0673-1
      1.Cookery, Japanese. 2.Sushi. I. Title

TX724.5.J3.I65 2003
641.5952--dc22   2003063405

Published by Sterling Publishing Co., Inc.
387 Park Avenue South, New York, NY 10016

© 2004 by Sterling Publishing Co., Inc.

Distributed in Canada by Sterling Publishing
C/o Canadian Manda Group, One Atlantic Avenue,
Suite 105
Toronto, Ontario, Canada M6K 3E7
Distributed in Great Britain by Chrysalis Books Group
PLC
The Chrysalis Building, Bramley Road, London W10
6SP, England.
Distributed in Australia by Capricorn Link (Australia)
Pty. Ltd.
P.O. Box 704, Windsor, NSW 2756, Australia

Printed in China
Sterling ISBN 1-4027-0673-1

In loving memory of my parents,
Ryoko and Keizo Imatani, who gave
me my first exciting taste of sushi.
And to my husband Srul and
daughter Danielle Ryoko—who share
my love of sushi today.

Con

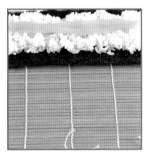

tents

When I first visited New York, I felt like I was walking into "Sushi City." Uptown. Downtown. There was sushi all over town—in restaurants, bars, groceries, fancy gourmet shops, corner delis, and even little take-out joints. There they were—those **little black-bottomed plastic trays** with the same clear covers filled with an assortment of sushi—some looking fresh and enticing, and some looking downright dry and unfriendly. Ick!

"Do people also make their own sushi?" I asked my friend Oscar, and he just laughed. "No way," he said. "Sushi is **In, gorgeous, delicious,** but you have to be a sushi master to make it, not a wimp like me! I don't know anyone who would dare make sushi at home except you, Aya!" **Coming from Japan, I didn't exactly know what a wimp was,** so Oscar explained. "A wimp could be a banker or a delivery boy...

it's just someone who's a little scared to take that first step, especially into the wide unknown—like sushi. Raw fish tastes great in a Japanese restaurant, and I'd really love to impress my friends, but make it at home? I wouldn't know where to begin!"

So there you have it: The reason I wrote this book. For all you Oscars and Richards, Susans and Sallys out there. I want to turn you all from Sushi Wimps into Sushi Wonders. Impress your friends. Tantalize your lovers. And give everyone a taste of my home—in your home.

In this book, you'll learn all the basics, step-by-step, just as if I'm standing there alongside of you. After all, sushi has been a part of my life since infancy. My father owned a sushi bar in Kobe, Japan, and while some children were playing with blocks, I filleted my first fish at the age of 5! Owning a sushi bar was a demanding business, and when my brother and I were little, our parents were often busy. But every night, after closing time, the two of us sat down at the bar just like grown-ups and Otosan (Father) made us whatever kind of sushi we asked for. Now that I've grown up and work in the restaurant business, I can really appreciate that special attention. For us, it made the hours of waiting worthwhile, and created a love and respect for sushi I share to this day.

When I was little, sushi bars in Japan were very expensive (some still are), so most people would only go there to celebrate a birthday, anniversary, or special event. The truth is, that most Japanese people are still a bit hesitant to go into a traditional sushi bar and order à la carte (mainly because the price list is nowhere in sight!). You could ask the sushi chef, but it isn't considered "cool" to ask. (Whoever invented that custom, I don't know).

Actually, even the managers of sushi bars are in favor of price lists, but some customers object, for fear that they might look "cheap." Since many of them are taking out business clients anyway, if the food is good and the mood is congenial, the price is right. So until recently, sushi bars in Japan were not places that students or young couples frequent like they do in America. Lucky you!

Lucky for us, things have changed drastically since the invention of kaitenzushi bars, what you might call the high-tech answer to sushi-for-everyone. In a kaitenzushi bar, the sushi is placed on plates on a conveyor belt, running all around the place. The color of the plate depends on the ingredients, and each color has a different price. "I'll take one of 100 yen, and two of 150," you might say, depending on how much you want to spend. And that's quite a relief, if you know what I mean. Kaitenzushi bars are everywhere, and since there's so much competition, owners know that if the sushi isn't fresh or if there's not enough variety, there's another bar just around the corner. When the first kaitenzushi bar was introduced, everyone was skeptical. Now they can eat their hat, and we can eat our sushi!

But don't think the standard sushi bars have disappeared. There are still those who have been in business for over 50 years. You'd be amazed at the elegance of the food served at these classic sushi bars, and the truth is that the taste and aesthetics can't be beat. There you can enjoy the harmony of the finest ingredients, and the best culinary skills Japan has to offer. If you're visiting Japan, don't miss the experience.

Today, I run a Japanese catering business, and I've served sushi to many people in many places throughout the world. But because I live outside Japan, most of my clients aren't Japanese. Do I serve different sushi to Japanese clients? Yes and no. It's important to me to get the best of what's in season for all my clients, and I try to give my Japanese clients the kind of sushi that they can't get in restaurants or bars. But I've also discovered that while the Japanese like their sushi arranged with exquisite design but elegant simplicity, many non-Japanese people look at the same "elegant simplicity" as a half-empty plate!

One of the greatest things about making your own sushi is developing your own personal style and aesthetics. Let your imagination soar.

Is sushi healthy? Science has shown that seaweeds do contain impressive amounts of protein, calcium,

B complex vitamins, the antioxidant vitamin A, and other vitamins and trace minerals (especially nori), in addition to everything we put on the sushi rice. But Japanese food can also be unhealthy if you choose poor ingredients or use too much sugar, salt, or oil. So remember—whatever you eat may be good for you or not, depending on the ingredients, the way you cook them, and even the way you eat.

The Origins of Sushi

Sushi is a very ancient art that was actually created as a way to preserve food. According to food historians, rice probably originated in Southeast Asia or China, and the people of Thailand and Laos fermented rice and fish as early as 500 B.C. In Japan the original process (in the Heian period 794–1185 A.D.) used only pickled fish or seafood, and when my ancestors finally did add rice in the 17th century, it was just to help the fermentation process—then the rice was actually discarded! It wasn't until the middle of the Edo period (1700 A.D.) that the ancients discovered the delicious aspects of vinegared rice, which entered into sushi history, and which we still enjoy today.

In this book, we'll start with the basics—everything you need to know before you begin: How to choose the right tools and tableware, and what a well-stocked Japanese pantry should have, with clear photos of each of the ingredients, so you'll already feel like a fish-in-water when you're selecting ingredients. Since I firmly believe that only the best and purest ingredients should go into making sushi, I've included easy recipes for how to make your own pickled ginger (it's also a lot less expensive), and even your own genuine wasabi—if you can get your hands on a root.

And to make sure you don't feel (or look) like a wimp, there are some really important tips on how to choose a whole fish or fillet—so you're sure you're getting the finest and the best. If you're adventurous or do your own fishing, there are even instructions for how to fillet a fish by yourself (that will really impress everyone!), but I'd practice once or twice before doing it before a live audience.

Sauces add lots of flavor to sushi, so next there are easy recipes for everything from sushi vinegar, to homemade teriyaki and spicy sauce. Then we move to making different kinds of sashimi, nigiri, gunkanmaki rice balls in nori, temaki hand rolls, thin hosomaki rolls, and a tempting array of all-vegetarian sushi, for all you veggie fans out there.

To accompany your sushi feast, there are two suggestions for the classic soups we start with. And last but certainly not least, are some of our most favorite family sushi treats that my mother used to make for our annual school sports festival in autumn, Girls' Day holiday in March, and other Japanese holidays and special days I remember as a child.

So *go for it,* Oscar—and all the rest of you out there. I just know you'll be glad you did.

Enjoy!
Aya

The *Basics*

Tools for the Sushi Master (or Mistress)

Having the right tools on hand makes it a lot easier and more enjoyable to make sushi, and while some—like a strainer, bowl, measuring cup, and plastic cutting board—you may already have, there are others that you might have to look for in Asian groceries, gourmet shops, and an increasing amount of supermarkets. Many are inexpensive, and some are optional. But for best results, I have to insist on using Japanese knives (info and tips below).

a. ELECTRIC RICE MAKER
Today virtually everyone in Japan uses an electric rice maker (in fact, most of them have forgotten how to cook rice without one!). Owning an electric rice maker is helpful, but certainly optional.

b. FINE WIRE MESH STRAINER
(Between 7" and 9") for straining cooked vegetables or removing bonito flakes from soup.

c. NORI STORAGE BOX
It's always a good idea to store nori in a storage box to prevent it from absorbing moisture. Use an airtight plastic box or a metal box with a good seal. Either one works fine.

d. PLASTIC OR WOODEN BOWL
(Between 12" and 15") for mixing rice with vinegar.

e. STAINLESS STEEL BOWL
For mixing sauces.

f. HONENUKI
Tweezer to remove fish bones.

g. HIBACHI
A compact little barbeque, used with charcoal for broiling seafood, and grilling eel, salmon, or tuna.

h. FRAME

For making Oshizushi (p. 116).

i. MAKISU
STANDARD BAMBOO SUSHI MAT

Although two kinds are sold, we want the type made with flat slats, usually green on one side. After using, brush out any stray pieces of rice. Rinse under running water with a little soap if desired, and dry thoroughly before storing. Never put a sushi mat in the dishwasher!

j. TEMAKI-YOU MAKISU
SUSHI MAT FOR TEMAKI (hand rolls)

About 5" x 5". Instructions for care are the same as for standard bamboo sushi mat. Wooden sushi paddle for transferring rice to hand roll.

k. TOISHI

Japanese knife sharpener. This is the best type of sharpener to sharpen Japanese knives. Always keep the stone submerged in water. (For best results, change water every week.)

l. KITCHEN TOWELS

Made of polyester, perfect for drying knives and wiping hands while working. Unlike terry towels, these towels do not leave fibers on the food or work surface.

m. MANAITA
PLASTIC CUTTING BOARD

Recommended size: 20" x 10", at least 1" thick. To avoid bacterial contamination, wipe with a little diluted bleach and place in the dishwasher.

n. GLASS SHAKERS

For Shichimi (Japanese chili pepper) and Irigoma (roasted sesame seeds).

o. PLASTIC DRESSING BOTTLE

For sauces.

p. JAPANESE KNIVES

Japanese knives are especially designed for the kind of food we want to prepare. Unlike stainless steel knives, authentic Japanese knives are made with a thin carbon steel blade that is sharper than the conventional stainless steel knife, and does less cell damage to the fish when you cut it. Check to see that the blade is firmly attached to the wooden handle. In this picture we see a long Sashimi Bouchou (p 1), used for slicing boneless fillets. The shorter knife (p 2) is Deba Bouchou—an all-purpose knife for filleting fish or chicken if it has bones.

There are many different lengths of knives. To choose the right one for you, lift the knife and feel the weight of it in your hand. If it's too heavy, try another one that's lighter. The blade should be about 12" long (without the handle). Wash the blade with soap and water and dry immediately to prevent staining or rust. If you don't use your knife often, oil it lightly and wrap it up in a towel. Store in a dry place.

NOTE: Japanese chefs never sharpen their knives just before using, because a freshly sharpened knife affects the delicate taste of fish. Always sharpen the day before you intend to use it.

h

i

j

k

l

m

n

o

p 1

p 2

Tableware

Imagine sushi as an actor and the garnish as its costume. The plate is its stage. If you use a plate that's too busy for serving sushi, you won't be able to see or enjoy the sushi clearly.

On the other hand, you don't really need to have a full set of traditional Japanese dishes to serve sushi, but using the right dishes certainly adds to the atmosphere. There are many places to buy Japanese-style tableware, but if you can't find them, use solid-colored plates in interesting shapes like squares or rectangles (circular plates are inappropriate for sushi).

Unlike Chinese food, which is served from a central serving dish, the Japanese set the table so that each person has his own utensils—including a place mat and individual soy sauce bowls. And don't crowd the table with flowers; in Japan, we practice Ikebana— the art of flower arranging—using one or two beautiful flowers that make their own statement. Candles are nontraditional.

a. SHOYUZARA
Dish for soy sauce.

b. TAMAKI-DAI
Stand for serving hand rolls.

c. HASHIOKI
Stand for chopsticks; **Hashi**—chopsticks.

d. SUSHIOKE
Traditional lacquer bowl for serving different kinds of sushi.

e. SASHIMIZARA
Dish for sashimi with a separate compartment for soy sauce (ceramic).

f. JAPANESE APPETIZER PLATE
Can also be used for serving sushi (ceramic).

a

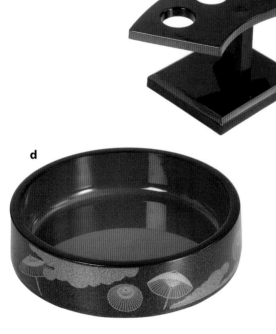

b

c

d

e

f

g. JAPANESE APPETIZER PLATE
Ceramic.

h. SHIRU-WAN
Wooden soup bowl for miso soup.

i. OCHOUSHI (bottle for sake)
& OCHOKO (cups for sake).

j. YUNOMI
Special green tea cup, for green tea
served along with sushi.

k. SHELL CERAMIC DISH
For soy sauce or other condiments.

l. KOZARA (one in front)
& KOBACHI (two in back)
Small dish for salad, arranged sashimi,
or condiments like pickles.

m. SASHIMI BUNE
Decorative wooden ship for serving
sashimi.

CHOPSTICKS:
NOT ALL ARE CREATED EQUAL

Chopsticks are the perfect complement to sushi—and wooden ones are the best to use. But not all chopsticks are created equal: The typical Japanese chopstick is 8" long and made of wood, with a thicker top and a thinner bottom. Koreans use the same shape, but made of silver. The Chinese use much thinner and longer (10") chopsticks made of bamboo, lacquered wood, or plastic, and unlike the Japanese, they often use a spoon to eat rice. Thai people use chopsticks shaped like the Chinese version, and frequently eat rice with a fork or spoon. Why the difference?

 I believe that the reason lies in the type of rice we eat—both Japanese and Koreans use a sticky type of rice, easy to pick up and transfer to the mouth with two sticks. But Chinese and Thai people eat a drier type of rice, which doesn't have that "adhesive" quality, making it far more practical to use a spoon for rice dishes—and chopsticks for everything else.

g

i

j

l

k

m

The Japanese Pantry

a. KEZURIBUSHI
Tinted dried bonito flakes, used mostly for soup.

b. NORI
You can judge a quality nori by its color: Good quality nori is black, cheaper kinds are green. To keep fresh after opening, store it in a nori box in a cool place. If you suspect your nori is less than fresh, or if you prefer the taste, toast it by holding the rough side over a flame for just a few seconds. I like to use leftover nori as a sauce for steamed rice: Cook 1/4 cup flaked nori, 2 tablespoons mirin, 1 tablespoon sugar, and enough soy sauce to cover the nori, over a low flame until thickened. Or cut leftover nori into strips with scissors, and use to garnish soups, fish, or vegetable dishes.

c. UMEBOSHI PLUMS
Small pink salted plums used as a condiment. Sold in boxes, bottles, or as a paste, umeboshi plums are believed to be effective in reducing fatigue, heartburn, and sore throats. Be careful of the pits!

d. GREEN TEA
In Japan, we always get a big cup of strong green tea when we sit down at the sushi bar. Like pickled ginger, green tea is used to refresh your mouth before eating and between bites. Sushi bars serve a variety of green teas like Sencha (regular green tea), Bancha (coarse green tea), and Konacha (powdered green tea). Sencha is a lightly toasted green tea with a fresher taste than the other types. A fine tea, it is also usually the most expensive. Bancha has a full-bodied flavor, and is moderately priced. While most restaurants serve Konacha tea because of its bright green color, the other types are preferable.

e. MIRIN
Japanese cooking wine made from rice. Store in a cool dark place after opening. If unavailable, use double the amount of sake and reduce by cooking to the amount required in the recipe.

f. WAKAME
One of the most popular seaweeds in Japanese cooking, wakame's mild flavor and soft texture make it very suitable for use in salads, soups, and stews. In Japan we buy it fresh from the fishmonger, but it's much easier to find it dried. To use, reconstitute by soaking in cold water and cover for at least an hour before use.

g. SOY SAUCE
There are many different kinds of soy sauce, but the best one to use for sushi is the Japanese type, of course! Chinese soy sauce is aged for a shorter time than traditional Japanese soy sauce, and may contain additives like sugar.

h. RICE VINEGAR
Rice vinegar is an integral part of sushi rice, and should not be substituted with any other kind of vinegar.

i. TAKUWAN
Pickled daikon (large white) radish. Used in sushi as a condiment or garnish.

j. BLACK SESAME SEEDS
Always toast in a dry frying pan before using. Used for garnish.

k. JAPANESE MAYONNAISE
Compared to the mayonnaise in other countries, Japanese mayonnaise has a slightly stronger mustard taste. Substitute regular mayonnaise with a little added mustard, if desired.

l. TOFU
A soy "cheese" made from soy beans, water and a starter, tofu is a low-calorie low-fat, high-protein food that the Japanese call "meat of the field." The quality of tofu depends on the water with which it is made. Once you open the package, store tofu in water to cover, and change daily. Keep refrigerated, and use within 3 days of opening.

m. MACCHA
Green tea used on special occasions and in the Japanese tea ceremony. Unlike other green teas, this type requires several steps in its preparation, which makes the ceremony that much more impressive!

n. DASHI NO MOTO
Soup stock made of kombu and fish—usually bonito flakes. While you can use many types of fish to make dashi, I never use sardines because of their strong smell and flavor.

o. INARI
Deep-fried tofu-pockets (Abura-age) that are cooked with mirin and sake. In Japan, we buy tofu-pockets in tofu shops and cook them at home, which I would recommend if there's a tofu shop in the city or town in which you live. If not, use canned.

p. POWDERED SUSHI VINEGAR

An instant product sold in individual sachets, powdered sushi vinegar is very popular in Japanese homes. To make sushi rice, just sprinkle a little on the rice while it's hot.

q. GARI

Pickled ginger is very easy and inexpensive to make at home. See p. 23 for recipe. Ginger is considered one of the oldest and healthiest spices, used in folk medicine throughout the world. In Japan we use ginger peels (from peeling fresh ginger) in tea, or candied in sugar. Try some ginger tea if you feel a cold coming on or to soothe a sore throat.

r. MISO

Miso is a fermented soybean product with a paste-like consistency. Although it is high in sodium, miso also contains B12 and enzymes beneficial for the digestive system (like yogurt). All types are made with soybeans, but some have the addition of wheat or barley. Some are light (like Shiro miso) and some are dark (Aka miso). I always like to mix both dark and light miso in soups. Miso can also be used for making pickles: For real Japanese pickles, we make a 1" layer of any kind of miso, a layer of firm vegetables like cucumber, radish, or carrots, and another layer of miso (sometimes mixed with a little mirin or soy sauce). Cover and refrigerate for 3 days before using. Will keep for up to one week.

s. KAMPYO

A type of Japanese pumpkin or gourd that is available dried in strips or tenderized and already seasoned.

t. DRIED SHITAKE MUSHROOMS

Large dark-brown mushrooms that are succulent and almost meat-like in texture. Although fresh shitake mushrooms are available in gourmet stores, we always use dried shitakes for sushi. To reconstitute them, soak them in warm water overnight. Remove the stems before use. Shitakes are very healthy—in addition to containing vitamins (like D, B12, and B2) and enzymes, they are considered to have healing qualities. Use leftover water for soups, tempura batter, and cooking fish. The mushrooms can also be used in vegetable stews, soups, sauces, and stir-fries.

u. DRIED KOMBU SEAWEED

Kombu is harvested from the deep, cold waters off northern Japan and is sun-dried on the beach before packaging. Mostly used for soup stock, reconstituted kombu is also used as a wrap for fish before cooking. Before using, wipe with a towel or brush to remove dust or sand.

p

r

s

t

u

The Wonders of Wasabi

WASABI POWDER

Wasabi is Japanese horseradish, made from an olive-green root with a bumpy skin. The best roots are more than 4 years old, which makes them quite expensive, even in Japan. Most people outside of Japan use powdered wasabi (which is actually made from a non-Japanese type of horseradish). To make wasabi from powder, add a small amount of boiling water to the powder (using boiling water makes the color very bright and brings out the "heat") and mix well. Let stand till room temperature. Although most people garnish plates with a little "hill" of wasabi, you can also shape it like playdough into a leaf or flower shape. Use within a short time or it will lose its "punch."

WASABI PASTE

There are many brands of wasabi paste, some (but not most) actually containing real wasabi! For best results, use wasabi paste manufactured in Japan. Wasabi paste is always preferable to powder.

REAL WASABI: BACK TO THE ROOTS

If you should happen to get your hands on a fresh wasabi root, you'll also need a shark's skin board to grind it on. You'll find one in an Asian grocery. Peel the root a couple of inches from the top. Hold the root from the bottom and scrape on the board in a slow circular motion (it will have a mucilagenous quality). Never use a grater—the wasabi will lose its heat and be chunky rather than smooth.

In Japan, we never add fresh wasabi to soy sauce like we do in the States. Instead, we put a little minced fresh wasabi on top of the fish, and then dip it in the plain soy sauce.

In a Pickle: How to Make Pickled Ginger

In the best restaurants and sushi bars, we always make our own pickled ginger, but many people prefer to buy it ready-made. I often find commercial pickled ginger to be too sweet or to have a chemical aftertaste, and you don't want to taint the taste of delicate sushi or sashimi with chemicals, do you?!

It's easy to make pickled ginger at home, but if you buy it ready-made, be sure to check the ingredients on the package before you buy.

q

GARI (Pickled Ginger)

Always look for fresh ginger that has as thin a skin as possible. The youngest ginger has skin that's almost translucent. Avoid pieces that look dry or shriveled. They will be tough and fibrous inside.

1 lb. fresh ginger
2 cups sushi vinegar (see recipe p. 36)
3 tablespoons salt

Wash and dry ginger. Peel and slice as thinly as possible. Discard any sprouted tips. Place ginger in a bowl and mix in the salt. Let stand 3 minutes. Rinse and drain to remove salt. Transfer to a nonreactive bowl or glass jar and pour over the sushi vinegar. Cover and let stand in a cool dark place (not in the refrigerator) for at least 1 week before using. Taste and add a little sugar if desired. May be stored indefinitely in the refrigerator, but ginger flavor will deteriorate after long storage.

Fish &

Seafood

How to Choose a Whole Fish

Many people (not only wimps but experienced gourmets!) are wary of buying whole fish, because they're afraid of getting stuck with something best fed to their cat. So here's my own tried-and-true method to empower you, so you'll never get stuck with something fishy!

STEP 1: Body Language
Check out the body of the fish. This is a good-looking fish; it has no scars or bruises and is moist.

1

This fish looks like it has seen better days. It is bruised and dry looking, and probably was lying around the shop for up to a week. This kind of fish can be cooked or fried, but should never be used for sushi.

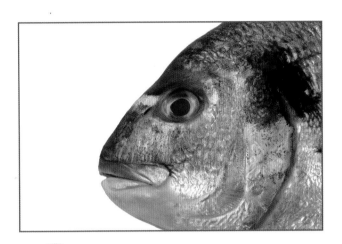

STEP 2: The eyes have it!
Look at the bright eye on this fish, and see how clear it is. He's perfect!

The eye of this fish has already started to turn brown, and it's hard to tell the iris apart from the white. This fish should not be used for sushi, but can still be used for cooked dishes.

STEP 3: Check out the fins:
The fins should be moist and undamaged, like on this fish.

The fins of this fish are separated and broken. This is a fish to avoid!

Glossary

There are an amazing number of fish that can be used to make sushi, but the way they taste depends not only on what kind of fish they are, but also on where and how they were raised. What's the difference? Throughout my travels around the world, I've discovered that commercially-bred fish just aren't as tasty as those that come from their natural environment—the sea. Sometimes they even have the smell and taste of the food they were raised on. It's amazing! Once I ate farm-raised madai—red snapper—that tasted exactly like sardines, and a friend revealed that the farm it came from indeed fed their fish sardines! In nature, fish can eat a variety of foods, but in farm-raised fish they're usually given the same feed everyday, and it makes a difference.

But not only feed is important; there's even a difference in taste according to climate. For example, the Japanese believe that natural madai from a warm climate with mild water currents will never be as tasty as one from a cold sea with wild currents, and that goes for other fish as well. Incidentally, red snapper could almost be called our Japanese National Fish, since it is always served at celebrations and happy ceremonies. Visually appealing, it is large, beautiful, and pink like a sakura (cherry) blossom, as well as mild and noble in taste. We Japanese adore it grilled, cooked, and for sashimi.

Since red snapper is also one of my favorite fish, I've tried it all over the world, and while in some places I've enjoyed it immensely, in other places I didn't like it at all! So my advice is, get friendly with a reputable fishmonger, and use seasonal, nonfarm-raised fish. You'll never look like a wimp if you carry this list in your pocket.

AKAMI
RED-COLORED FILLETS

Chutoro (Medium Fatty Tuna)
In Japan, it is considered a gourmet choice.

Katsuo (Bonito Tuna)
Like a sardine, bonito tuna has a slightly stronger smell and taste. For balance, the Japanese eat it with strong flavors like scallions, ginger, garlic, and seasoned soy sauces.

Maguro (Tuna)
This is one of the most popular fish for sushi: low-fat and high-protein. Yellowfin or bluefin lean cut tuna are the kinds usually used for sushi. It's best to experiment with maguro sushi in the winter, when the tuna is at its peak.

Ootoro (Fatty Tuna)
Like french fries, ootoro is very popular among young people and kids because of its oily taste and texture.

HAKARIMONO
SILVERY FISH

All the fish in this category have a slightly stronger smell and taste, so we season or marinate them first before using them for sushi.

Aji (Horse Mackerel)
Serve with ginger, scallions, and a squeeze of yuzu orange or lime juice and soy sauce.

Iwashi (Sardine)
Follow instructions for Aji. Note: Since it's impossible to remove all the tiny bones, only serve this to someone who won't mind! (The bones are rich in calcium anyway.)

Saba (Mackerel)
We never eat mackerel raw. Always salt it first, rinse, and marinate in vinegar before serving.

Sayori (Halfbeak)
This fish is the mildest tasting of the group.

NIMONO
STEAMED FISH & SEAFOOD

Anago (Sea Eel or Sea Conger)
Lighter colored and more delicate flavor and texture than unagi (eel).

Ebi (Shrimp)

Geso (Cuttlefish Tentacles)
A rounder, thicker, and chewier relative of the squid (calamari). Lean and nutritious.

Hamaguri (Large Clam)
Used for nigiri.

Tako (Octopus)

Unagi (Eel)
In Japan, we usually use anago with sushi, and unagi for serving with plain rice.
But outside of Japan, people love it for sushi.

SEAFOOD

Akagai (Ark Shell)
One of my favorites!

Ama Ebi (Sweet Shrimp)
With a slightly sweeter taste. Served raw.

Aoyagi (Surf Clam)
Slightly chewy taste.

Awabi (Abalone)
Always used raw for sashimi and steamed for sushi.

Ebi odori (Shrimp)
Served raw.

Ebikko (Shrimp Roe)

Hotate (Scallop)
Mild taste and character.

Ika (Cuttlefish)

Ikura (Salmon Roe)
Orange-red shiny balls. The name ikura derives from "ikra," a word used in Russia and throughout the Mediterranean for fish roe or caviar, or a salad made with it.

Kazanoko (Herring Roe)
Yellow roe chunks, a seasonal winter specialty; somewhat expensive.

Tobbiko (Flying Fish Roe)
Tiny, bright-orange eggs, loose and crunchy. Can be prepared as nigiri or maki sushi and is often used for garnishing the outside of hand rolls.

Torigai (Cockle Clam)

Uni (Sea Urchin)
A delicacy in many parts of the world, uni is actually the gonads of the sea urchin. It has a delicious, subtle, nut-like flavor that is popular among advanced sushi eaters.

SHIROMI
WHITE-COLORED FILLETS

Engawa (Special Fillet of Flounder taken from the stomach area)
Slightly fatty, this is considered a gourmet choice with a special flavor. Consequently, it is also much more expensive than regular flounder fillets.

Hamachi (Yellowtail)
Slightly fatty taste. Look for the smaller fish (or fillets from a smaller fish) because they will be less fatty.

Hiramachi (Amberjack)
Tastes like yellowtail but is far less fatty.

Hirame (Flounder)
One of the best choices for sushi, with a mild taste and almost no smell.

Kurodai (Sea Bream)
Similar to red snapper, but with more tender flesh.

Madai (Red Snapper)
One of the best choices for sushi and any Japanese dish.

Shima-Aji (Yellowjack)
Slightly fatty taste. Beware—sometimes Aji (horse mackerel), which is less expensive, is sold as yellowjack (which is more expensive). Make sure you're getting what you pay for!

Suzuki (Sea Bass)
There are both sweet water (kawa suzuki) and saltwater varieties. The saltwater variety is always better.

Choosing a Fillet

Many people buy ready-cut fillets. But how do you know you're not getting a raw deal?

Check It Out:
Take a look at both these salmon fillets. One was frozen and defrosted, the other one is fresh. Sometimes, disreputable stores will sell frozen fish as fresh. How do you know the difference? The one on the left (which was frozen) has a dull, frosted color, while the fresh fillet on the right has a bright, clear color and fibers that can be seen clearly.

Check It Out:
Now look at these two tuna fillets. The one on the left is very fibrous on the outside. This will be tough and should be avoided. The other one has a nice clear color and no fibers are visible. This is the one to choose.

You Can Do It!
How to Fillet a Whole Fish

Step 1:
Have the fish scaled and the viscera and stomach removed by the fishmonger. Using a Deba Boucho or other sharp knife, I cut through the flesh just behind the gills, cut or break the backbone at the cut, and remove the head.

Step 2:
Next, I chop off the tail and remove the fins on the back and stomach side, and any small fins near the head.

Step 3:
The fish is dressed. (Or undressed. It depends on how you look at it!)

Step 4:
Now we get down to serious business: I place the fish on its side, and insert the knifepoint through the top of the back, and then use the whole blade in gentle sawing motions to cut through one side of the back to the center bone, drawing it down to the middle of the fish.

Step 5:
I turn the fish over and do the same thing starting from the tail side up to the middle. (This will create one fillet.)

Step 6:
For the other fillet, I repeat step 4, cutting through to the other side of the center bone.

Step 9:
With the fingers of my left hand on the back of the fish and the stomach part facing away from me, I insert the knife and cut the fish from top to bottom, without cutting through the skin.

Step 7:
Same as step 5.

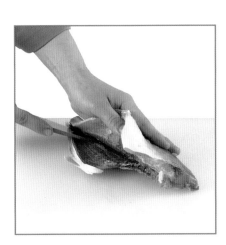

Step 10:
Inserting the knife slightly at an angle, I slide the knife along the skin to push it away from the center.

Step 8:
Now I open the fish, skin side down, and remove the stomach bone.

Step 11:
Now that I've removed one fillet, I turn the fish around and remove the other one. Remove any remaining bones in the fillets, wash, and pat dry.

Now, wasn't it easier than you thought it would be?!

Sauces

How to Make Sushizu
Sushi Vinegar

Sushi vinegar makes or breaks the taste of sushi rice. In fact, another term for sushi in Japanese is "shari neta," "shari" meaning rice, and "neta" fish and seafood. You'll notice the word "rice" comes first, because if you spoil the rice, the fish and seafood will be disappointing!

INGREDIENTS:

4 cups rice vinegar
6 tablespoons sugar
2 tablespoons salt
2 tablespoons sake
1 piece kombu (1" x 3")

2 Heat on a low flame, stirring constantly with a wooden spoon, just until the sugar and salt are dissolved.

1 Pour vinegar, sugar, and salt into a saucepan.

3 Cool to room temperature and add the kombu and sake. Pour into a mason or other jar with a cover. Keep out of sunlight in a cool dark place (refrigeration unnecessary). Keeps indefinitely.

Tsukuri Jyouyu
Special Soy Sauce for Sashimi

Although most restaurants serve sashimi with plain soy sauce, in Japan we always serve it with Tsukuri Jyouyu, which is actually a blend of soy sauce and mirin rice wine. The mirin adds a special aroma to the soy sauce, enhancing the taste of the plain fish.

INGREDIENTS:
½ cup mirin
4 cups soy sauce
1 piece kombu (1" x 3")

1. Pour mirin into a saucepan and bring to a boil over high heat. Stir in the soy sauce and cool to room temperature.

2. Pour into a bottle, add kombu, and close tightly. Store in a cool dark place for up to one year.

Karashisumiso

This is a great sauce for seafood sushi and sashimi, and a typical dressing for steamed vegetable salads. It's really easy to make, and stores indefinitely in the refrigerator.

INGREDIENTS:
4 tablespoons miso (shiro miso is preferable)
1 tablespoon prepared mustard
4 tablespoons sushi vinegar
1 tablespoon yuzu (Japanese lime) or lime juice

1. Mix the miso and mustard together and add the vinegar and lime juice.

2. Beat with a wire whisk till smooth. Pour into a glass jar and store in the refrigerator. Shake before using.

Teriyaki Sauce

Everybody loves Teriyaki sauce, but in Japan, it's far less popular than it is around the world. Actually, "teri" means shine or glaze, and "yaki" means grill, which gives you some idea of why and how we use it. Outside of Japan, people often use it for both marinating and grilling foods, but it can also be used as a dipping sauce. While Teriyaki sauce is sold everywhere, the best kind is the one you make at home.

INGREDIENTS:
1 cup mirin
1 cup sake
4 tablespoons sugar
1 cup soy sauce (do not use light soy sauce)

1 Pour the mirin and sake into a saucepan and bring to a boil over high heat. Slowly pour in the sugar, and stir with a wooden spoon till the sugar is dissolved. Lower heat and cook for 1 hour. Add the soy sauce to the pan and continue to cook for an additional 30 minutes over low heat.

2 Pour into a bottle, cover tightly, and store in a cool dark place or in the refrigerator.

Spicy Sauce

Spicy sauce is not Japanese. It is a purely American invention that was created especially for those of you who like a little "kick" in your sushi. Some people love this sauce on salads and boiled seafood, chicken, or other mild-tasting foods.

INGREDIENTS:

5 tablespoons Japanese mayonnaise or regular mayonnaise

1 tablespoon tomato paste

1 teaspoon raayu (sesame oil with chilli)

A few drops soy sauce or to taste

Put the mayonnaise in a bowl, and add a few drops of soy sauce. Blend with a wire whisk.

Add tomato paste and raayu and mix well.

Cover and store in the refrigerator, or transfer to a plastic dressing bottle.

Sashimi

Introduction

If you ask anyone from Japan what his favorite type of sushi is, he'll answer "Sushi? No Sushi. Sashimi!" because we like sashimi best of all. The word "sashimi" comes from the words "sa" meaning knife and "shi" meaning "fillet," so basically what it is, is just a sliced fillet. You always have to use the best of the best for making sashimi, since the flavors aren't "interrupted" by rice or other ingredients except the sauce or condiment served on the side.

If you were to go into a sushi bar in Japan, you'd almost always see the natives ordering sashimi first, and sushi only afterwards. Sashimi goes especially well with alcohol—and not only sake—like Japanese beer, shouchou (Japanese spirits), or dry white wine.

Outside of Japan, I've frequently seen sushi bars serving freshwater fish just as they would any other kind of sashimi, something you'll never find in Japan! In fact, if I was working in Japan and dared to make a regular sashimi portion from a freshwater fish, I'd lose my job! The reason is, in Japan—where we have become accustomed to such an excellent variety of natural cold saltwater fish—people think that raw freshwater fish smells and tastes like mud. Instead of regular sashimi, we prepare it "arai" ("washed")—cutting it as thin as possible, always dipping it in ice water, and serving it with a sauce made of vinegar and miso.

And a word about salmon: Although salmon (sake sashimi) is one of the most popular choices in sushi bars around the world, in Japan it didn't really catch on until recently. The reason is that compared with our other wonderful fish, salmon was considered to have a heavy taste and strong odor. When they did make it, Japanese sushi chefs always chose to use thin slices from the part of the fillet that's near the tail, where it is less fatty and has a milder smell. (It's not that we don't like the taste of fatty fish—it's just that fatty salmon didn't appeal to us.)

Tastes have changed in Japan, and today people eat sake sashimi like they do in the rest of the world. In fact, thick slices of fattier salmon called Beni Toro are now more expensive than lean tuna! But when I use salmon for sashimi, I still do what my father taught me—use the tail end of the fillet. You'll also find it's easier to slice thinly.

In this chapter, I'd also like to introduce types of sashimi not typically found in sushi bars. You can't imagine how many ways you can enjoy sashimi!

How to Slice a Fillet for Sashimi

I like to use a Sashimi Bouchou knife for this one, but
any good, large, sharp knife will also do.

1 Gently hold the fillet with your left hand. Make sure to curl your fingers under (so they don't become sashimi too).

2 Cut into 3/8" slices according to recipe directions.

3 This is a typical sashimi platter, with maguro (yellowfin tuna).

Sashimi Vegetables

Sashimi vegetables serve the same function as wasabi or ginger—they refresh your mouth between bites. Decoratively cut, they also add an aesthetic touch to the plate.

The most typical vegetables used to garnish sashimi are radishes (daikon white radish or red radish), (hothouse) cucumbers, lettuce, and fresh shiso leaves, which are sometimes cut into intricate designs. Other possibilities are finely grated carrot, parsley, scallions, and oshinko (pickled radish). Use your imagination, but don't go overboard!

1 For an easy cucumber garnish, hold a small hothouse cucumber on its side, and use a knife to peel off lengthwise strips.

 Slice the cucumber thickly.

For an easy red radish garnish: Slice unpeeled radish very thinly, and line up the slices with edges overlapping.

Other garnish possibilities:

a. Ruby loose-leaf lettuce

b. Thinly grated carrots (check out the special grater found in Asian supermarkets)

c. Parsley (in the background) and julienned radish (in the foreground)

d. Thinly sliced hothouse cucumber and carrot crown (in the background), sliced cucumber (in the foreground).

e. Oshinko—sliced three different ways

f. Scallions—cut off at the root, the base in thin, lengthwise slices, and placed in ice water to curl the bottom into a flower shape.

Arranged Maguro Sashimi
Tuna

This impressive-looking sashimi is really easy to make, once you get the knack of rolling it up. Just remember to overlap the slices, make sure the filling is neatly packed inside, and roll up firmly. I also give you another variation I like, using sake (salmon) and salmon roe. It reminds me of a delicate spring flower.

INGREDIENTS FOR 1 PORTION:
6–8 slices of maguro (tuna) $\frac{1}{8}$" thick
8 matchstick slices of oshinko
1 piece nori, 7" x 1"
White sesame seeds (for garnish)

1 Arrange the slices in a line with the edges overlapping. Place the oshinko pieces in a bunch at the beginning of the line. Carefully begin rolling from the bottom up, using the fingers to keep the maguro slices in place. Roll tightly.

2 Wrap a band of nori around the base to keep the sashimi in place.

VARIATION:

Sake Sashimi

Salmon

Here's another variation on the theme, using ten slices of sake sashimi. In this one, I don't use oshinko in the middle: After I roll up the salmon, I carefully fold back the edges, spreading them out slightly like a rose, and fill the middle with about a teaspoon of salmon roe. Garnish with snipped chives and serve on a bed of thinly sliced lemon.

Kawa Suzuki Arai
Freshwater Bass

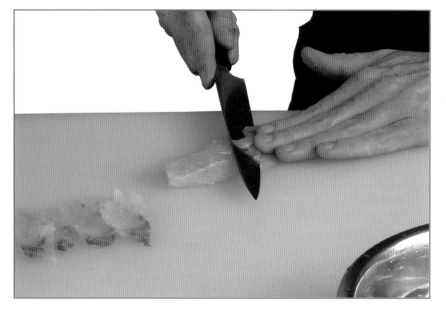

INGREDIENTS:

8–10 slices of suzuki (freshwater bass), cut paper-thin

Ice water

1½ tablespoons chopped scallions (green part only)

Bowl of crushed ice and Karashisumiso sauce for serving

1 Hold the fillet with your left hand, keeping fingers straight, instead of curled under. Position the knife at a slight angle (so you don't slice your fingers as well!), and slice the fish paper-thin, using a slight back-and-forth sawing motion.

2 Drop the slices into a bowl of ice water. Use a chopstick to help separate the slices. Let stand for 3–5 minutes. The fillets will shrink slightly.

3 Arrange on top of crushed ice and garnish with chopped scallions. Serve with Karashisumiso sauce.

Takosumiso
Sliced Octopus

In Japan, we most like to eat octopus steamed in green tea with the addition of sake or rice vinegar (sake gives it a milder taste, but vinegar helps the color stay bright). I suggest using Bancha green tea, found in every health food store.

Believe it or not, the octopus that you eat as sashimi in a sushi bar probably came from an octopus about 30" long that weighed more than 10 lbs.! Since you probably don't want to deal with such a large octopus in your kitchen (it might not even fit into the sink!), ask your fishmonger to suggest what size of tentacle is necessary for the number of portions you wish to make.

INGREDIENTS FOR 10 TAKOSUMISO PORTIONS:
1 lb. cleaned octopus tentacles
Salt
1 Bancha tea bag
4 cups water
1 tablespoon sake or rice vinegar

For serving:
Sliced hothouse cucumbers
Karashisumiso sauce or wasabi & soy sauce

1 Rinse tentacles and massage with salt. Rinse again under running water, paying special attention to the suckers. Place the tea bag, water, and sake or vinegar in a large saucepan and bring to a boil. Add the tentacles and cook uncovered over low heat for 10 minutes. Remove the tea bag and let the octopus come to room temperature in the water. Rinse gently under running water and slice into 1" chunks.

2 Place in a bowl and garnish with sliced cucumbers. Serve with wasabi and soy sauce, or Karashisumiso sauce (my favorite!).

Sushi Rice

Sushi Rice

Now that we've seen how to make sashimi, we move on to sushi—the basis of which is sushi rice. Although as I mentioned before, most people and many sushi bars in Japan use electric rice cookers, I still believe that the best way to prepare sushi rice (or any rice, for that matter) is by cooking it yourself, especially over a flame.

Don't gasp. This recipe makes a lot of sushi rice, because the truth is, it just doesn't have the correct balance of flavors if you make a smaller amount. We also take into account that we discard about 15 percent of the cooked rice—especially around the edges and bottom of the pot where the grains are harder. Actually, if you divide the mixture between nigiri, hand rolls, and other types of sushi, it's the perfect amount for an average dinner or cocktail party, with no rice leftovers.

My father taught me to always buy from this year's stock of rice ("shinmai"), because it will be moister and more flavorful than older rice, and therefore need less water in preparation. If possible, check the package when you buy rice to see if it has the manufacturing date printed on the wrapper. (In some Asian groceries, you can also buy rice in bulk, so make sure to ask for "shinmai".) Older rice is drier, and will require slightly more water.

INGREDIENTS:

4 cups Japanese short-grain (sushi) rice
4 cups water
½ cup sushi vinegar

1. Place rice in a heavy-bottomed pot and rinse with running water.
2. Drain rice.
3. Add the 4 cups of water and soak for 30 minutes.
4. Cover with a tight-fitting lid and bring to a boil.
5. Keep cooking on high heat for 15 minutes with lid on.
6. Lower heat to a minimum and cook covered for 10 minutes.
7. Remove from heat, remove lid, and let sit undisturbed for 5 minutes.

NOTE: Always moisten your hands in a water-vinegar solution before shaping sushi rice. (See Nigiri tips, p. 56.)

This quantity of rice can be used for:
110 pieces of Nigiri or Gunkanmaki rice balls in nori
Or 30 Temaki hand rolls
Or 20 thin Hosomaki rolls
Or 12 Saimaki (inside-out) rolls
Or 8 Futomaki (traditional thick) rolls

1 Transfer the hot rice to a large shallow bowl, discarding any hard grains around the sides or bottom. Pour over the sushi vinegar.

Now we want the temperature of the rice to cool down quickly so that the grains of rice don't get too sticky. To do that we fan the rice (today an electric fan on medium speed often replaces the paper fan).

2 As you cool down the rice, use a wooden paddle to gently but constantly fold the mixture, just as you would if you were folding whipped egg whites into a cake batter. Don't stop until the rice cools down to room temperature, or you'll have to use your sushi rice for cement.

3 Here's the finished product. If you've followed the directions completely, it should have a nice sheen and be only slightly sticky.

Nigiri

Nigiri

Nigiri, which originated in the city of Tokyo, is the most popular type of sushi ordered in Japanese restaurants, and is always there among the sushi selections sold around town. The word "nigiri" means "squeeze" in Japanese, and nigiri is made by gently squeezing small amounts of sushi rice into small rectangular shapes, and topping them with bite-sized pieces of fish or other foods.

The most important thing is to create harmony between the rice and the flavor and size of the topping. In Japan, we also define a good nigiri as one that doesn't fall apart when you transfer it from the plate to your mouth, but is tender when it meets your tongue!

NIGIRI TIPS:

1. Prepare a bowl of water with a 30% rice-vinegar solution to dip your hands in before you pick up the rice. That way, the rice won't stick!

2. Practice makes perfect: Take a ball of rice and squeeze it gently in your hand to form a rectangular shape. Don't squeeze or play around with it too much, or the rice will lose the correct texture. Taste a little and check the firmness of the rice ball; as I mentioned before, it should be tender but not fall apart when lifted.

Here are 4 different kinds of nigiri from left to right:
Kurodai (Sea Bream)
Shima-Aji (Yellowjack)
Sake (Salmon)
Maguro (Tuna)

Looks good enough to eat!

Maguro Nigiri
Tuna

For this nigiri, you can use either yellowfin or bluefin tuna. Bluefin tuna has a meatier texture.

INGREDIENTS FOR 1 PIECE:
1 slightly rounded tablespoon sushi rice
½ oz. yellowfin or bluefin tuna fillet,
2–3" long, 1" wide, ⅛" thick

1 Moisten hands with water-vinegar mixture. Hold a small ball of sushi rice in your right hand. Squeeze gently into a rectangular shape.
   Pick up and hold a small fillet of tuna in your left hand.

2 Bring the rice ball to the fillet.

3 Use the thumb and forefinger of your right hand to gently press in the sides of the sushi, and use the thumb of your left hand to gently press it down at the top (which is really the bottom of the upside-down nigiri). Use your right hand to turn the pressed nigiri over in your left hand.

4 Now do the same thing in reverse—use the thumb and forefinger of your right hand to press in the sides. Use the thumb of your left hand to press the fish and rice together gently. There you have it!

Ebi Nigiri
Shrimp

INGREDIENTS FOR 1 PIECE:
1 slightly rounded tablespoon sushi rice
1 boiled peeled and butterflied shrimp (recipe follows)

2 Bring the rice ball to the shrimp. Use the thumb and forefinger of your right hand to gently press in the sides of the nigiri, and use the thumb of your left hand to press it down at the bottom (of the upside-down nigiri). Use your right hand to turn the pressed nigiri over in your left hand.

1 Moisten hands in the water-vinegar mixture and pick up a small ball of sushi rice in your right hand. Squeeze gently into a rectangular shape. Pick up and hold a butterflied shrimp in your left hand.

3 Use the thumb and forefinger to press in the sides, and two fingers of your right hand to press the shrimp and rice gently together topside.

Here are two kinds of ebi nigiri—with and without a nori band.

How to Boil & Butterfly Jumbo Shrimp

It's really easy to boil and butterfly your own shrimp in just minutes if you follow the process below. You'll note we always skewer the shrimp to help keep it from shrinking and losing its shape.

INGREDIENTS FOR 5 FRESH JUMBO SHRIMPS:

3 quarts water

1 cup rice vinegar

1. Remove the head of the shrimp and insert a long bamboo skewer through the middle—starting from the top and working it through in the direction of the tail.

2. Use your thumb to press and flatten the center of the tail section, to allow more space for the skewer to exit.

Bring the water and vinegar to a rolling boil, add the skewered shrimp, and cover the pot. Immediately remove from heat and let stand 3 minutes. Remove the shrimp and let cool to room temperature. Peel the shrimp and set aside.

3. Use the point of a sharp knife (like a Sashimi Boucho) to slit open the stomach from top to bottom, making sure not to cut all the way through. Gently open the shrimp and flatten. Repeat with the remaining shrimp.

Unagi Kabayaki Nigiri
Steamed & Teriyaki-Broiled Eel

INGREDIENTS FOR I PORTION:
I slightly rounded tablespoon sushi rice

3–4" long, I" wide piece broiled unagi (recipe follows)

I band nori 4" long, ½" wide

1 Moisten hands with water-vinegar mixture. Hold a small ball of sushi rice in your right hand. Squeeze gently into a rectangular shape. Pick up and hold a small fillet of eel in your left hand.

2 Use your right hand to place the unagi fillet on the rice (to avoid getting our hands dirty from teriyaki sauce!).

3 Place the nori band around the nigiri. Help them stick to each other by lightly moistening the edges of the band.

Here it is ready.
Mmmm.

How to Prepare Unagi Kabayaki
Teriyaki-Broiled Eel

INGREDIENTS:

1 x 10" long fresh eel fillet
5 bamboo skewers
1 cup teriyaki sauce (see recipe p. 38)

To begin:
Put the sticks widthwise through the side of the fillet 2" apart from each other. Cover and steam in a steamer basket placed over boiling water for 10 minutes. Remove and bring to room temperature. (Do not remove the skewers.)

1 Here's what the fillet looks like after steaming. Note the color.
Place the eel in a glass or nonreactive baking dish and brush with teriyaki sauce.
Grill over low coals (or on a hibachi) for 3–5 minutes, brushing with teriyaki sauce each time the fillet looks dry (which is often).

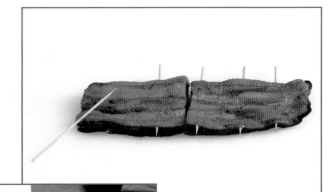

2 Here's what the fillet looks like after grilling. It should be shiny and glazed on top. Check out the color.

3 Gently remove the skewers from the fillet.

4 Slice widthwise into 1" pieces.

Tamago Nigiri
Japanese Omelette

The original tamago (Japanese omelette) was nothing like the sweet omelette served in sushi bars today. Made of white-meat fish pureed with eggs, mirin, sake, and bonito flakes—it had a different texture and only a very delicate sweetness.

For this nigiri, I include a recipe for a modern tamago that uses dried bonito flakes instead of fresh fish, and is still far closer to the original version than anything you'll find in your local sushi bar (see recipe following).

INGREDIENTS FOR 1 PIECE (with nori band):
1½ slightly rounded tablespoons sushi rice
1 slice of Tamago omelette (3–4" long, 1½" wide, ¼" thick)
1 band nori 4" long, ½" wide

Serve either or both kinds of Tamago Nigiri with wasabi and ginger.

Moisten hands with water-vinegar mixture. Hold a small ball of sushi rice in your right hand. Squeeze gently into a rectangular shape. Pick up and hold a slice of tamago in your left hand, and bring the rice to the tamago.
Use your right hand to turn the pressed nigiri over in your left hand.
Now place the nori band on top and fasten the edges under the rice.
Arrange on a serving plate and garnish with wasabi and ginger.

How To Make Dashimaki Tamago (Japanese Omelette)

The traditional Japanese omelette pan is an impressive-looking 9" square made of copper, but in homes today, most people use a 7" x 5" rectangular Teflon-coated pan. If you don't have one, use a 10" round skillet and trim the edges of the omelette once it's cooked.

Since the process of making a real tamago is a little tricky, you might want to make "crepes" ⅛" thick, trim the edges, and fold them as outlined in Step 10.

NOTE: Tamago omelettes can only be cooked over a gas stove. If yours is electric, give these instructions to a friend (or buy ready-made tamago).

INGREDIENTS FOR A 5" LONG, 3" WIDE, 1" HIGH OMELETTE (20 Nigiri portions):
6 large eggs
¼ cup water
2 tablespoons sake
1 tablespoon kezuribushi (dried bonito flakes) or 1 teaspoon dashi no moto
1½ tablespoons sugar
2–3 drops soy sauce
Corn or sunflower oil for frying

Arranged Tamago Nigiri
Japanese Omelette

This attractive-looking Tamago Nigiri is traditionally made with a pinch of sakura denbu (sweet cod powder) on top for a garnish.

INGREDIENTS FOR I PIECE:
1½ slightly rounded tablespoons sushi rice
1 slice tamago 3"–4" long, 1½" wide, ¾" thick
1 pinch sakura denbu, for garnish

1 Moisten hands with water-vinegar mixture. Using a sharp knife, cut the tamago lengthwise down the center, but not all the way through. (You'll notice that I suggested placing chopsticks on both sides of the tamago, to make sure it was not cut all the way through!).

Make a small ball of sushi rice in your right hand. Squeeze gently into a rectangular shape.

2 Gently place the nigiri rice in the middle of the omelette. Garnish with a pinch of sakura denbu.

1. Place water and sake in a saucepan and bring to a boil over high heat.

2. Add kezuribushi, stir, and remove from heat.

3. Strain through a wire-mesh strainer and discard the kezuribushi.

4. Add sugar to the water-sake (dashi) mixture and mix well until dissolved. Bring to room temperature.

5. In a bowl, whisk together eggs till light and fluffy.

6. Add cooled dashi and a few drops of soy sauce and mix well.

7. Strain the egg-dashi mixture so it is very smooth.

8. Lightly grease the omelette pan and heat over medium heat.

9. Pour just enough egg-dashi mixture into the pan to form a thin crepe. Use chopsticks to press out any air bubbles.

10. When slightly dry on the top, run chopsticks around the edges to loosen them. Now comes the tricky part: Imagine the omelette is divided by horizontal lines into thirds, the first third being the farthest away from you. Use chopsticks to fold ⅓ of the omelette from the far side towards the center. Now fold these ⅔ in your direction over the remaining ⅓.

11. Pour a little more egg-dashi mixture in the empty side of the pan, lifting the cooked omelette to let it flow underneath.

12. Repeat Step 11 and then Step 10 till tamago is 1" thick.

13. Remove tamago from pan and tighten with a bamboo sushi mat (makisu). Let chill to room temperature, and remove the makisu.

14. Cut into strips.

Personally, I think the name of this sushi is kind of
weird, since "gunkan" means battleship, which is
kind of a funny name to use for sushi. But actually,
this oval rice ball with nori wrapped around it does
look a little like a boat, but I prefer to think of it
as a sailboat—sailing off to some exotic destination.

Gunkanmaki

Ikura Gunkanmaki
Salmon Roe

INGREDIENTS FOR 1 PORTION:
1 slightly rounded tablespoon sushi rice
1 gunkan nori band (⅛ sheet = 7" x 1")
1 teaspoon salmon roe
2 thin slices hothouse cucumber, cut in half

Moisten hands with water-vinegar mixture. Hold a small ball of sushi rice in your right hand. Squeeze gently into a rectangular shape—like you did for nigiri. Place on a work surface. Attach one end of the nori to the middle of the rice ball.

1

Keep wrapping the nori around, making sure to keep it equidistant from the bottom.

2

Gunkanmaki ready for toppings.

3

Stand three of the cucumber half-slices up on the back of the gunkanmaki, and place the ikura on top. Garnish the plate with wasabi and ginger.

4

Ebikko Gunkanmaki
Shrimp Roe

Moisten hands with water-vinegar mixture. Hold a small ball of sushi rice in your right hand. Squeeze gently into a rectangular shape, just like you did for nigiri. Place on a work surface. Attach one end of the nori to the middle of the rice ball. Keep wrapping the nori around, making sure to keep it equidistant from the bottom.

INGREDIENTS FOR I PORTION:

I slightly rounded tablespoon sushi rice

I gunkan nori band (⅛ sheet = 7" x 1")

I teaspoon shrimp roe

2 thin slices hothouse cucumber, cut in half

Stand up three of the cucumber half-slices on the back of the gunkanmaki, and place the shrimp roe on top.

Garnish the plate with wasabi and ginger.

Maguro & Uzura Gunkanmaki
Tuna & Quail Egg

For those of you unfamiliar with them, quail's eggs are tiny brown-and-white speckled eggs that you can find in gourmet stores and Asian markets.

INGREDIENTS FOR I PORTION:
1 slightly rounded tablespoon sushi rice
1 gunkan nori band (1/8 sheet = 7" x 1")
1 teaspoon chopped tuna fillet
1 quail's egg yolk

1 Moisten hands with water-vinegar mixture. Hold a small ball of sushi rice in your right hand. Squeeze gently into a rectangular shape like you did for nigiri, and place on a work surface. Attach one end of the nori to the middle of the rice ball. Keep wrapping the nori around, making sure to keep it equidistant from the bottom. Now the gunkanmaki is ready for topping.

2 Place chopped tuna on top. Press down center of tuna gently with your finger.

3 Gently separate the egg, and place the yolk on the center of the tuna.

4 Garnish the plate with wasabi and ginger.

Spicy Tuna Gunkanmaki

1 Moisten hands with water-vinegar mixture. Hold a small ball of sushi rice in your right hand. Squeeze gently into a rectangular shape. Place on a work surface. Attach one end of the nori to the middle of the rice ball. Keep wrapping the nori around, making sure to keep it equidistant from the bottom.

Chop the tuna fillet and mince the scallion.

INGREDIENTS FOR 1 PORTION:
1 slightly rounded tablespoon sushi rice
1 gunkan nori band (⅛ sheet = 7" x 1")
1 teaspoon chopped tuna fillet
⅓ teaspoon minced scallion
½ teaspoon of spicy sauce (see recipe p. 39).

2 Mix the chopped tuna and minced scallion together with your fingers or a chopstick and place on the gunkanmaki. Press down lightly with your finger to flatten.

3 Add spicy sauce on top of gunkanmaki and garnish plate with wasabi and ginger

Grilled Tuna Salad Gunkanmaki

Unlike for sashimi, you can use up a chewier part of the tuna fillet for the salad.

INGREDIENTS FOR 1 PORTION:

1 slightly rounded tablespoon sushi rice
1 gunkan nori band (⅛ sheet = 7" x 1")
1½ teaspoons Tuna Salad (recipe follows)

For the Tuna Salad:

½ cup grilled tuna chunks
⅛ cup thinly sliced onion
2 tablespoons Japanese or regular mayonnaise

Prepare the ingredients for Tuna Salad.

Mix all ingredients together for the salad.

Moisten hands with a water-vinegar mixture. Hold a small ball of sushi rice in your right hand. Squeeze gently into a rectangular shape and place on a work surface. Attach one end of the nori to the middle of the rice ball. Keep wrapping the nori around, making sure to keep it equidistant from the bottom.

Gently place 1 teaspoon of prepared Tuna Salad on top of gunkanmaki. Garnish plate with ginger and wasabi.

Spicy Shrimp Gunkanmaki

The winning combination of shrimp, avocado, and spicy sauce make this a very popular gunkanmaki!

INGREDIENTS FOR I PORTION:
I slightly rounded tablespoon sushi rice
I gunkan nori band (⅛ sheet = 7" x 1")
I boiled shrimp, chopped
½ teaspoon chopped avocado
½ teaspoon of spicy sauce

1 Moisten hands with water-vinegar mixture. Hold a small ball of sushi rice in your right hand. Squeeze gently into a rectangular shape and place on a work surface. Attach one end of the nori to the middle of the rice ball. Keep wrapping the nori around, making sure to keep it equidistant from the bottom.

Mix shrimp and avocado together and place on top of gunkanmaki.

2 Pour spicy sauce on top of gunkanmaki.

3 Garnish plate with wasabi and ginger.

Negi Shima-Aji Gunkanmaki
Yellowjack & Scallion

INGREDIENTS FOR 1 PORTION:
1 slightly rounded tablespoon sushi rice
1 gunkan nori band (⅛ sheet = 7" x 1")
1 teaspoon chopped yellowjack fillet
⅓ teaspoon minced scallion

1 Moisten hands with water-vinegar mixture. Hold a small ball of sushi rice in your right hand. Squeeze gently into a rectangular shape, like you did for nigiri. Place on a work surface. Attach one end of the nori to the middle of the rice ball. Keep wrapping the nori around, making sure to keep it equidistant from the bottom.

Mix chopped yellowjack fillet and scallion, and gently place on top of gunkanmaki.

2 Garnish plate with wasabi and ginger.

Kani & Ebikko Gunkanmaki
Shrimp Roe & Crab Salad Salad

INGREDIENTS FOR I PORTION:

I slightly rounded tablespoon sushi rice

I gunkan nori band (1/8 sheet = 7" x 1")

1½ teaspoon Kani & Ebikko Salad (recipe follows)

For the Kani & Ebikko Salad:

1/3 cup Kanikama flaked crab or imitation crab (surimi)

I tablespoon shrimp roe

I tablespoon minced chives

I tablespoon Japanese or regular mayonnaise

Prepare the ingredients for the Kani & Ebikko Salad.

Mix all the ingredients together for the salad.

Moisten hands with water-vinegar mixture. Hold a small ball of sushi rice in your right hand. Squeeze gently into a rectangular shape and place on a work surface. Attach one end of the nori to the middle of the rice ball. Keep wrapping the nori around, making sure to keep it equidistant from the bottom.

Place the Kani & Ebikko Salad on top of the gunkanmaki, and garnish plate with wasabi and ginger.

Temaki means "hand roll" in Japanese, and in Japan, this is a popular sushi to make at home. Because it loses its texture very quickly, the best kind is made and served as fast as possible (not like in some restaurants!).

Temaki

Unatama Temaki
Broiled Eel, Tamago & Seasoned Shitake Mushrooms

This temaki blends broiled eel and tamago—the famous Japanese omelette—with fabulous seasoned shitake mushrooms. For instructions on how to make tamago, check out my recipe (see p. 62). Directions for seasoned shitakes follow.

INGREDIENTS FOR 1 PORTION:
½ sheet nori (7" long x 4" wide)
4 tablespoons sushi rice
2 pieces (1" x 3" each) fillet Unagi Kabayaki (Teriyaki-Broiled Eel, see recipe p. 61)
1 piece Tamago (Japanese omelette), 1½" x 3"
2 thin sticks hothouse cucumber (with peel)
1 Seasoned Shitake Mushroom, cut in half or into thin strips

Seasoned Shitake Mushrooms

As you read in The Japanese Pantry (p. 20), shitake mushrooms are very healthy (in addition to being delicious). In Japan, we use dried shitakes for flavoring soup and all kinds of other dishes, especially in the Zen kitchen, where they are slow-cooked in soy sauce and mirin and used as a meat substitute. They have a stronger aroma than fresh shitakes. When buying dried shitakes, always choose thick, meaty-looking ones.

We also use fresh shitakes of course, especially for salads, in tempura, and grilled or sautéed with salt and pepper.

INGREDIENTS FOR 1 PORTION:
3½ oz dried shitake mushrooms
1 cup water
2 tablespoons sugar
2 tablespoons mirin
2 tablespoons sake
4 tablespoons soy sauce

Brush the shitakes to remove any dust and loose pieces. Place in a bowl with the water, cover, and let soak overnight.

Drain and place mushrooms in a small saucepan. Add water to just cover and bring to a boil.

Add sugar, sake, and mirin and cook until reduced by half. Add soy sauce and continue cooking till sauce evaporates.

Moisten hands with water-vinegar mixture. Hold the sushi rice in your right hand. Place the nori in your left hand, and spread the rice on half the sheet (the side with your fingers).

Place all the rest of the ingredients for the filling on the diagonal.

Use the fingers of your right hand to fold the bottom right-hand corner of the nori over the filling.

Fold the bottom left-hand corner and bring it up to the upper right-hand corner.

Tighten the cone if necessary, and check to see that it can be placed in a temaki stand without falling apart.

Place in a temaki stand and garnish with wasabi and ginger.

Negi Maguro Temaki
Scallion & Tuna

"Negi" means scallion in Japanese, and "maguro" is, of course, tuna. (In Japan, we love to eat most of our fish and seafood with scallions.)

INGREDIENTS FOR 1 PORTION:
½ sheet nori (7" long x 4" wide)
4 tablespoons sushi rice
5" x ½" tuna fillet
1 teaspoon chopped scallion

Moisten hands with water-vinegar mixture. Hold the sushi rice in your right hand. Place the nori in your left hand, and spread the rice on half the sheet (the side with your fingers). Place all the rest of the ingredients for the filling on the diagonal.

Here's a close-up of the ingredients for anyone unsure of the correct placement. Now, use the fingers of your right hand to fold the bottom right-hand corner of the nori over the filling. Fold the bottom left-hand corner and bring it up to the upper right-hand corner. Tighten the cone if necessary and check to see that it can be placed in a temaki stand without falling apart.

Place in a temaki stand and garnish with wasabi and ginger.

New Age Temaki

The next three temakis are the result of a totally foreign invasion. All were invented in America (so was spicy sauce) but are popular today among young people in Japan. Although you'll never catch a Japanese gourmet eating one (at least not in public), you'll find them in most sushi bars in America and Europe.

California Temaki
Shrimp, Crab Salad & Asparagus

Make sure to use very young (slim) asparagus for this recipe, or cut off the bottoms of thicker asparagus, and peel the stem before you steam them.

INGREDIENTS FOR 1 PORTION:
½ sheet nori (7" long x 4" wide)
4 tablespoons sushi rice
1 boiled shrimp
1–2 steamed asparagus spears
1 teaspoon Kani & Ebikko Salad (see recipe p. 73)

1 Moisten hands with water-vinegar mixture. Hold the sushi rice in your right hand. Place the nori in your left hand, and spread the rice on half the sheet (the side with your fingers). Place all the rest of the ingredients for the filling on the diagonal.

Place the nori in your left hand, and spread the rice on the finger side of the sheet (half the sheet). Place all the rest of the ingredients for the filling on the diagonal.

3 Place in a temaki stand and garnish with wasabi and ginger.

2 Here's a closer look at the correct placement of ingredients on rice. Use the fingers of your right hand to fold the bottom right-hand corner of the nori over the filling. Fold the bottom left-hand corner and bring it up to the upper right-hand corner. Tighten the cone if necessary and check to see that it can be placed in a temaki stand without falling apart.

Hokkai Temaki
Salmon, Avocado & Cucumber

"Hokkai" means North Ocean in Japanese, and this temaki reflects our belief that the best fish come from the cold waters of the north.

INGREDIENTS FOR I PORTION:
½ sheet nori (7" long x 4" wide)
4 tablespoons sushi rice
5" long x ½" wide salmon fillet
5" long x ½" wide stick-sliced avocado (in one or two pieces)
5" long x ½" wide (hothouse) cucumber stick

1 Moisten hands with water-vinegar mixture. Hold the sushi rice in your right hand. Place the nori in your left hand, and spread the rice on half the sheet (the side with your fingers).
Place all the rest of the ingredients for the filling on the diagonal.

3 Place in a temaki stand and garnish with wasabi and ginger.

2 Use the fingers of your right hand to fold the bottom right-hand corner of the nori over the filling. Fold the bottom left-hand corner and bring it up to the upper right-hand corner. Tighten the cone if necessary and check to see that it can be placed in a temaki stand without falling apart.

Norwegian Temaki
Salmon, Grilled Salmon & Salmon Roe

A triple salmon experience, starring raw salmon fillet, grilled salmon, and salmon roe—this temaki is a true gourmet treat!

Moisten hands with water-vinegar mixture. Hold the sushi rice in your right hand. Place the nori in your left hand, and spread the rice on half the sheet (the side with your fingers). Place all the rest of the ingredients for the filling on the diagonal except for the salmon roe.

Use the fingers of your right hand to fold the bottom right-hand corner of the nori over the filling. Fold the bottom left-hand corner and bring it up to the upper right-hand corner. Tighten the cone if necessary and check to see that it can be placed in a temaki stand without falling apart. Garnish with salmon roe.

Place in a temaki stand and garnish with wasabi and ginger. What a beautiful sight!

INGREDIENTS FOR 1 PORTION:

½ sheet nori (7" long x 4" wide)

4 tablespoons sushi rice

5" x ½" salmon fillet

1 teaspoon grilled flaked salmon

5" long x ½" wide stick–sliced avocado (in one or two pieces)

½ teaspoon spicy sauce

⅓ teaspoon salmon roe

Hosomaki is a "thin roll" filled with one or two kinds of ingredients. Although it looks simple, it's somewhat more difficult to make, because the ingredients have to look good and fit together snugly, and the roll needs to be neatly done. Follow the instructions and pictures carefully, and I bet you'll get it on the first try!

Hosomaki

Tekka Maki
Tuna

Tekka means "metal fire," probably the reason this sushi is so popular among the macho crowd in Tokyo!

INGREDIENTS FOR 1 ROLL (6 PIECES):
½ sheet nori (7" long x 4" wide)
6 tablespoons sushi rice
7" long x ½" wide tuna fillet

1 Place the nori on a sushi mat. Moisten hands with water-vinegar mixture and flatten the rice on top, leaving ½" from the bottom and sides. Place the tuna fillet in the middle of the rice.

2 Place your thumbs under the bottom of the sushi mat, and use the remaining fingers to hold the filling in place.

3 Bring the mat up to cover the filling, leaving ½" from the top edge of the nori, and enclose the roll.

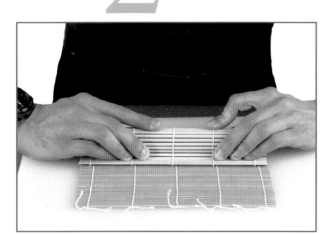

4 Press firmly with the fingers to tighten the roll, then raise the cover and bring forward slightly. Now close again over the entire roll firmly and remove the cover. (This seals the edge.)

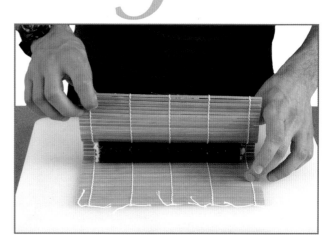

5 This is how the roll should look. Does yours look this way?
Slice the roll in half, and then each half into 3 pieces. Arrange on a serving platter with wasabi and ginger.

sushi for wimps

Ebikyu Maki
Shrimp & Cucumber

This hosomaki is a special favorite among my friends, who enjoy the crisp taste of the cucumber ("Kyu" comes from Kyuri, which means cucumber), together with the simple but succulent taste of boiled shrimp (ebi).

INGREDIENTS FOR 1 ROLL (6 PIECES):

½ sheet nori (7" long x 4" wide)

6 tablespoons sushi rice

2 boiled shrimps

7½" hothouse cucumber stick (in 1 or 2 pieces)

¼ teaspoon sesame seeds, toasted in a dry frying pan

1 Place the nori on a sushi mat. Moisten hands with water-vinegar mixture and flatten the rice on top, leaving ½" from the bottom and sides. Place the boiled shrimp and cucumber in the middle of the rice. Sprinkle the sesame seeds on top.

2 Here is how it looks with all the ingredients correctly lined up. Now place your thumbs under the bottom of the sushi mat, and use the remaining fingers to hold the filling in place. Bring the mat up to cover the filling, leaving 1" from the top edge of the nori, and enclose the roll. Press firmly with the fingers to tighten the roll, then raise the cover and bring forward slightly. Now close again over the entire roll firmly and remove the cover. (This seals the edge.)

3 Slice the roll in half, and then each half into 3 pieces. Arrange on a serving platter with wasabi and ginger.

Unakyu Maki
Eel & Cucumber

1. Place the nori on a sushi mat. Moisten hands with water-vinegar mixture and flatten the rice on top, leaving 1/2" from the bottom and sides. Place the eel and cucumber in the middle of the rice. Sprinkle the sesame seeds on top. Now place your thumbs under the bottom of the sushi mat, and use the remaining fingers to hold the filling in place. Bring the mat up to cover the filling, leaving 1/2" from the top edge of the nori, and enclose the roll. Press firmly with the fingers to tighten the roll, then raise the cover and bring forward slightly. Now close again over the entire roll firmly and remove the cover. (This seals the edge.)

INGREDIENTS FOR 1 ROLL (6 PIECES):

1/2 sheet nori (7" long x 4" wide)

6 tablespoons sushi rice

1 1/2" x 7" fillet Unagi Kabayaki (Teriyaki-Broiled Eel, see recipe p. 61)

7 1/2" hothouse cucumber stick (in 1 or 2 pieces)

1/4 teaspoon sesame seeds, toasted in a dry frying pan

2. Slice the roll in half.

3. Then slice each half into 3 pieces.

4. Arrange on a serving platter with wasabi and ginger.

Sake Maki
Salmon

INGREDIENTS FOR I ROLL (6 PIECES):
½ sheet nori (7" long x 4" wide)
6 tablespoons sushi rice
7" long x ½" wide salmon fillet

1. Place the nori on a sushi mat. Moisten hands with water-vinegar mixture and flatten the rice on top, leaving ¹/2" from the bottom and sides.

2. Place the fillet salmon in the middle of the rice. Now place your thumbs under the bottom of the sushi mat, and use the remaining fingers to hold the filling in place. Bring the mat up to cover the filling, leaving 1" from the top edge of the nori, and enclose the roll. Press firmly with the fingers to tighten the roll, then raise the cover and bring forward slightly. Now close again over the entire roll firmly and remove the cover. (This seals the edge.)

3. Slice the roll in half, and then each half into 3 pieces. Arrange on a serving platter with wasabi and ginger.

Hokkai Maki
Salmon & Avocado

Place the nori on a sushi mat. Moisten hands with water-vinegar mixture and flatten the rice on top, leaving $1/2$" from the bottom and sides. Place the salmon and avocado in the middle of the rice.

INGREDIENTS FOR 1 ROLL (6 PIECES):
$1/2$ sheet nori (7" long x 4" wide)
6 tablespoons sushi rice
7" long x $1/4$" wide salmon fillet
$7 1/2$" avocado stick (in 1 or 2 pieces)

Now place your thumbs under the bottom of the sushi mat, and use the remaining fingers to hold the filling in place.

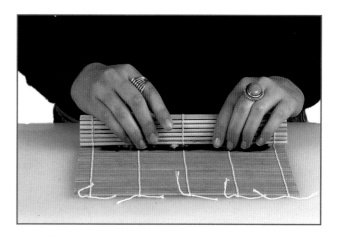

Bring the mat up to cover the filling, leaving 1" from the top edge of the nori, and enclose the roll. Press firmly with the fingers to tighten the roll, then raise the cover and bring forward slightly. Now close again over the entire roll firmly and remove the cover. (This seals the edge.)

Slice the roll in half, and then each half into 3 pieces. Arrange on a serving platter with wasabi and ginger.

Tamago Maki
Japanese Omelette

1 Place the nori on a sushi mat. Moisten hands with water-vinegar mixture and flatten the rice on top, leaving 1/2" from the bottom and sides. Place the Tamago in the middle of the rice.

INGREDIENTS FOR I ROLL (6 PIECES):
1/2 sheet nori (7" long x 4" wide)
6 tablespoons sushi rice
7" long x 1/2" wide slice Tamago
Pinch of sesame seeds, toasted in a dry frying pan

3 Place your thumbs under the bottom of the sushi mat, and use the remaining fingers to hold the filling in place. Bring the mat up to cover the filling, leaving 1" from the top edge of the nori, and enclose the roll. Press firmly with the fingers to tighten the roll, then raise the cover and bring forward slightly. Now close again over the entire roll firmly and remove the cover (this seals the edge).
Slice the roll in half, and then each half into 3 pieces.

2 Sprinkle over the toasted sesame seeds.

4 Arrange on a serving platter with wasabi and ginger.

Inside-out rolls (Saimaki)—made with the rice placed first on the sushi mat and the ingredients arranged on top of the nori—are very popular around the world, but haven't really caught on in sushi bars in Japan. Although they look very complicated to make, they're really very easy if you follow the directions. Remember—the order of placing the ingredients on the nori always depends on their texture: things that are sticky (like mayonnaise) are put on first, and only then the fish and other ingredients—that way you don't end up making a gooey mess out of it all!

Saimaki

Magurotaku Saimaki
Tuna & Pickled Radish

Cover makisu (sushi bamboo mat) on both sides with plastic wrap. Moisten hands with water-vinegar mixture and cover the top of the mat with a layer of flattened sushi rice (it should be the same size or slightly larger than the nori we'll put on next). Place nori on a sushi rice. Arrange all the ingredients in the middle of the nori, except for the sesame seeds. Check to see if your ingredients are lined up like they are in this picture.

INGREDIENTS FOR 1 ROLL (6 PIECES):

½ sheet nori (7" long x 4" wide)

8 tablespoons sushi rice

7" long x ½" wide tuna fillet

7" long x ½" wide stick Takuwan (pickled daikon radish)

7½" hothouse cucumber stick (in 1 or 2 pieces)

3 tablespoons toasted black sesame seeds

Now place your thumbs under the bottom of the sushi mat, and use the remaining fingers to hold the filling in place. Bring the mat up to cover the filling, leaving 1" from the top edge of the nori, and enclose the roll. Press firmly with the fingers to tighten the roll, and then raise the cover and bring forward slightly. Now close again over the entire roll firmly and remove the cover. (This seals the edge.)

Sprinkle the black sesame seeds in a flat dish or platter and gently roll the saimaki in the seeds.

Slice the roll in half, and then each half into 3 pieces. Arrange on a serving platter with wasabi and ginger.

California Saimaki
Shrimp, Asparagus & Cucumber

1 Cover makisu (sushi bamboo mat) on both sides with plastic wrap. Moisten hands with water-vinegar mixture and cover the top of the mat with a layer of flattened sushi rice (it should be the same size or slightly larger than the nori we'll put on next). Place nori on the sushi rice. Arrange all the ingredients, except for the shrimp roe, in the middle of the nori.

INGREDIENTS FOR 1 ROLL (6 PIECES):

½ sheet nori (7" long x 4" wide)

8 tablespoons sushi rice

3 boiled shrimp

7½" hothouse cucumber stick (in 1 or 2 pieces)

7½" steamed asparagus (1 or 2 pieces)

2 tablespoons Kani & Ebikko Salad (see recipe p. 73)

1 tablespoon shrimp roe

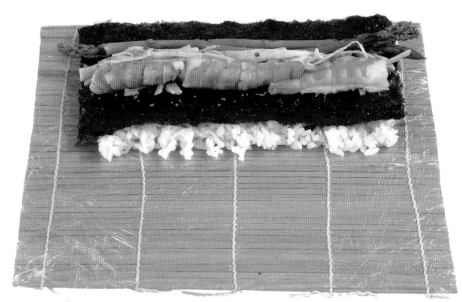

2 This is how to line up the ingredients.

Place your thumbs under the bottom of the sushi mat, and use the remaining fingers to hold the filling in place. Bring the mat up to cover the filling, leaving 1" from the top edge of the nori, and enclose the roll. Press firmly with the fingers to tighten the roll, and then raise the cover and bring forward slightly. Now close again over the entire roll firmly and remove the cover. (This seals the edge.) Slice the roll in half, and then each half into 3 pieces.

Place shrimp roe in a flat dish. Pick up each piece individually and dip into the shrimp roe.

Arrange on a serving platter with wasabi and ginger.

Norwegian Saimaki
Salmon, Avocado & Scallion

Having someone special over for dinner tonight? You're sure to impress him/her with this—a rich combination of sushi rice, two kinds of salmon, avocado, and scallions on the inside, artfully wrapped with salmon fillet wrapper on the outside. Some people even call it a salmon lover's dream.

First we make the regular saimaki roll, and then replace the plastic wrap and sushi mat, and squeeze it gently to put on the salmon wrapper. Don't worry—you'll get it!

INGREDIENTS FOR I ROLL (6 PIECES):

½ sheet nori (7" long x 4" wide)

8 tablespoons sushi rice

Ruby lettuce

2 teaspoons Japanese or regular mayonnaise

½ teaspoon minced scallion

2 tablespoons grilled flaked salmon

7" long x ½" wide salmon fillet (for the filling)

7" long x ½" wide avocado stick (in one or two pieces)

7" long x 4–5" wide thin-sliced (⅛") salmon fillet (for the wrapping)

1 Cover makisu (sushi bamboo mat) on both sides with plastic wrap. Moisten hands with water-vinegar mixture and cover the top of the mat with a layer of flattened sushi rice (it should be the same size or slightly larger than the nori we'll put on next). Place nori on the sushi rice. Place a leaf or two of lettuce in the center of the rice, and using a plastic squeeze bottle filled with mayonnaise, make a horizontal line of mayo in the middle. Sprinkle on the scallions, and arrange the flaked salmon, salmon fillet, and avocado stick on top.

Now place your thumbs under the bottom of the sushi mat, and use the remaining fingers to hold the filling in place.

Bring the mat up to cover the filling, leaving 1" from the top edge of the nori, and enclose the roll. Press firmly with the fingers to tighten the roll, and then raise the cover and bring forward slightly. Now close again over the entire roll firmly and remove the cover. (This seals the edge.)

Now comes the tricky part: Transfer the saimaki roll to a clean cutting board and cover the top with the remaining salmon fillet. Place a clean piece of plastic wrap on top, and cover with the makisu. Gently squeeze to attach the fillet to the top and sides of the roll. (It will cover three-quarters of the roll. It doesn't have to cover the underside.)

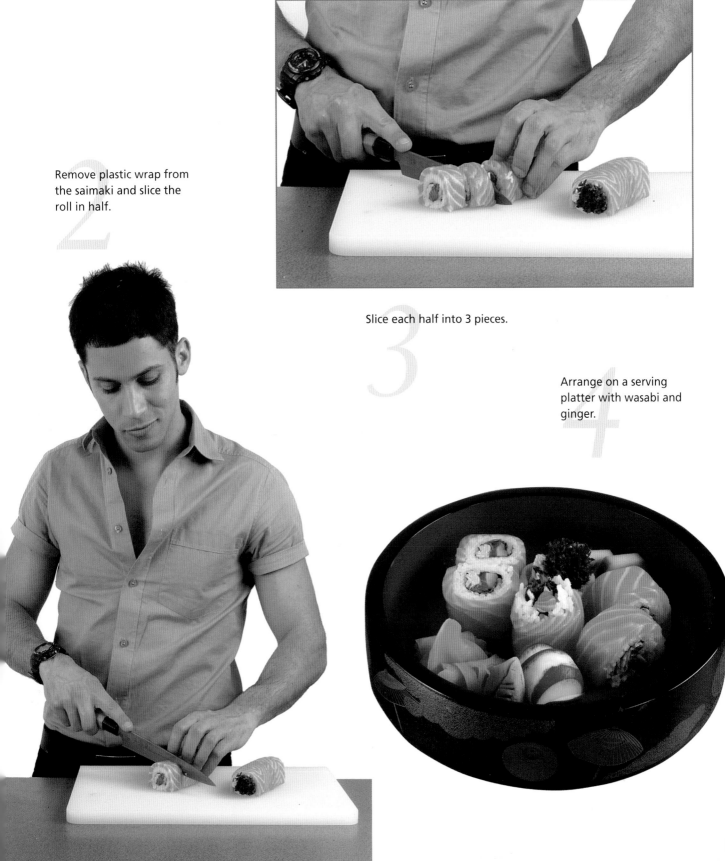

Remove plastic wrap from the saimaki and slice the roll in half.

2

Slice each half into 3 pieces.

3

Arrange on a serving platter with wasabi and ginger.

4

Futomaki (Traditional Thick Roll)
Shrimp & Broiled Eel

Although this isn't an inside-out roll, I've added the recipe to this chapter because, like saimaki, it is a thick roll with many ingredients. In Japan we use sea conger—sea eel—for making futomaki, but since it's more difficult to find, I suggest using unagi—freshwater eel—instead. This recipe demonstrates the principle of preparing futomaki. Please feel free to experiment with your favorite ingredients.

INGREDIENTS FOR 1 ROLL (6 PIECES):

1 sheet nori

12–14 tablespoons sushi rice (a little more than ¾ cup)

7" long x 1" wide Unagi Kabayaki (Teriyaki-Broiled eel, see recipe p. 61)

3 boiled shrimp

7" long x 1" wide Tamago (see recipe p. 62)

2 Seasoned Shitake Mushrooms, cut in half or into thin strips (see recipe p. 76)

2 tablespoons steamed spinach

1 teaspoon sakura denbu (sweet cod fish flakes)

½ teaspoon sesame seeds, toasted in a dry frying pan

1 Place the nori on a sushi mat. Moisten hands with water-vinegar mixture and flatten the rice on top, leaving 1" from the bottom and sides. Arrange all the ingredients on the rice. This is how to line up the ingredients.

2 Now place your thumbs under the bottom of the sushi mat, and use the remaining fingers to hold the filling in place. Bring the mat up to cover the filling, leaving 1" from the top edge of the nori, and enclose the roll. Press firmly with the fingers to tighten the roll, and then raise the cover and bring forward slightly. Now close again over the entire roll firmly and remove the cover (this seals the edge).

3 Slice the roll into 6 pieces. (Or better yet, slice the roll in half, and each half into 3 pieces.)

4 Arrange on a serving platter with wasabi and ginger.

All Veg

These days, there are many sushi-lovers who prefer to eat vegetarian food, or order vegetarian sushi as part of their selection. Whether for health or humane reasons, or just to add a pleasing crunch, veggie sushi provides a touch of color and aesthetic harmony to any sushi selection.

etarian Sushi

Shitake Maki
Shitake Mushrooms

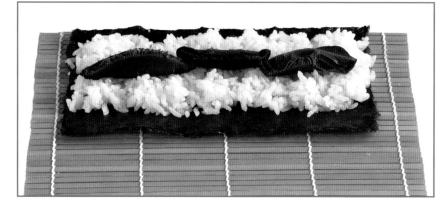

INGREDIENTS FOR 1 ROLL (6 PIECES):

½ sheet nori (7" long x 4" wide)

6 tablespoons sushi rice

1 Seasoned Shitake Mushroom, cut in half or into thin strips (see recipe p. 76)

Pinch of toasted sesame seeds

1 Place the nori on a sushi mat. Moisten hands with water-vinegar mixture and flatten the rice on top, leaving 1" from the bottom and sides. Place the shitake mushroom in the middle of the rice. Sprinkle over the toasted sesame seeds. This is how to line up the ingredients.

2 Now place your thumbs under the bottom of the sushi mat, and use the remaining fingers to hold the filling in place. Bring the mat up to cover the filling, leaving 1" from the top edge of the nori, and enclose the roll. Press firmly with the fingers to tighten the roll, and then raise the cover and bring forward slightly. Now close again over the entire roll firmly and remove the cover. (This seals the edge.)

Slice the roll in half, and then each half into 3 pieces.

3 Arrange on a serving platter with wasabi and ginger.

Oshinko Maki
Pickled Radish

Most people think that "Oshinko" means pickled daikon, but the word really refers to all kinds of pickles, which we Japanese love to prepare at home. Pickling was among the earliest forms of food preservation not only in Japan, but around the world.

INGREDIENTS FOR 1 ROLL (6 PIECES):
½ sheet nori (7" long x 4" wide)
6 tablespoons sushi rice
7" long ½" wide Takuwan (pickled radish)
Pinch of toasted sesame seeds

1 Place the nori on a sushi mat. Moisten hands with water-vinegar mixture and flatten the rice on top, leaving ½" from the bottom and sides. Place the Takuwan in the middle of the rice. Sprinkle on the toasted sesame seeds.

2 Now place your thumbs under the bottom of the sushi mat, and use the remaining fingers to hold the filling in place. Bring the mat up to cover the filling, leaving 1" from the top edge of the nori, and enclose the roll. Press firmly with the fingers to tighten the roll, and then raise the cover and bring forward slightly. Now close again over the entire roll firmly and remove the cover. (This seals the edge.)
Slice the roll in half, and then each half into 3 pieces.

3 Arrange on a serving platter with wasabi and ginger.

Aspara Maki
Asparagus

Although asparagus aren't native to Japan, they've been lovingly adopted by the Japanese. We still haven't given them a Japanese name, however!

INGREDIENTS FOR 1 ROLL (6 PIECES):

½ sheet nori (7½" long x 4" wide)

6 tablespoons sushi rice

2 7"-long steamed thin asparagus spears or 1 thick one (peeled)

Pinch of toasted sesame seeds

1 Place the nori on a sushi mat. Moisten hands with water-vinegar mixture and flatten the rice on top, leaving ½" from the bottom and sides.

2 Place the asparagus in the middle of the rice. Add toasted sesame seeds.

Now place your thumbs under the bottom of the sushi mat, and use the remaining fingers to hold the filling in place. Bring the mat up to cover the filling, leaving 1" from the top edge of the nori, and enclose the roll. Press firmly with the fingers to tighten the roll, and then raise the cover and bring forward slightly. Now close again over the entire roll firmly and remove the cover. (This seals the edge.)

Slice the roll in half, and then each half into 3 pieces.

3 Arrange on a serving platter with wasabi and ginger.

Saishoku Saimaki
Mixed Vegetables

Saishoku means vegetarian in Japanese, and this saimaki is an especially healthy feast for vegetarians and nonvegetarians alike. In addition to contrasting textures (like avocado and carrot), it contains so many vitamins and minerals it's hard to count. Like the Norwegian saimaki, this roll has a "wrapper" around it—made of avocado instead of salmon—which gives it a delightful taste and unique "look." Don't feel you have to make the recipe exactly as written—feel free to experiment with other vegetables and/or with regular or seasoned tofu.

INGREDIENTS FOR 1 ROLL (6 PIECES):

½ sheet nori (7" long x 3½" wide)

8 tablespoons sushi rice

7" long x ½" wide piece Takuwan

7" long x ½" wide avocado stick (in one or two pieces)

1 tablespoon steamed leaf spinach, well drained

7" long hothouse cucumber stick

7" long carrot stick

1–2 Seasoned Shitake Mushrooms, cut in half (see recipe p. 76)

Pinch of toasted sesame seeds

For the wrapping:

Enough 5" long x 1/8" thick avocado slices to cover the roll

Bring the mat up to cover the filling, leaving 1" from the top edge of the nori, and enclose the roll. Press firmly with the fingers to tighten, then raise the cover and bring forward slightly. Now close again over the entire roll firmly and remove the cover. (This seals the edge.)

Place the Saimaki on a cutting board. Drape the thin avocado slices over the roll (it should cover all but the bottom of the roll). Gently cover the roll with plastic wrap and replace the bamboo mat. Press the roll gently but firmly to help the avocado adhere to the rice. Remove the mat and plastic wrap from the Saimaki. Slice the roll in half, and each half into 3 pieces.

Cover Makisu (sushi bamboo mat) with plastic wrap. Moisten hands with water-vinegar mixture and flatten the sushi rice on top (it should be the same size as the piece of nori). Place nori over the sushi rice, and lay all the ingredients in the middle of the nori, like you see in this picture. Add toasted sesame seeds.

Now place your thumbs under the bottom of the sushi mat, and use the remaining fingers to hold the filling in place.

Arrange on a serving platter with wasabi and ginger.

Soups

Misoshiru
Miso Soup

About Miso Soup...

The first time I walked into a sushi bar in New York, I was really surprised to see everyone sipping the same kind of miso soup with little tofu cubes and wakame in it. In fact, every Japanese restaurant that I visited in America seemed to serve the same kind of soup. Why was I surprised? Because in Japan, this is never done. While miso soup may be an integral part of a sushi meal, it is always served with fish or seafood. The kind served in America—with tofu and seaweed—traditionally goes with other types of meals.

Miso soup is like an espresso coffee—it's not the kind of soup that improves in taste the longer it is heated; it just becomes very salty. (In fact, boiling miso soup destroys the beneficial enzymes it contains.) So it's better to make or heat the amount you want just before serving.

If you use dashi no moto (instant fish soup powder), check the flavor before you buy; it comes in various flavors like pure bonito, pure sardine, or mixed bonito and sardine. For serving with sushi, you'll want to have pure bonito because of its mild flavor. For serving with teriyaki or other Japanese meals, sardine or mixed sardine-bonito is fine.

INGREDIENTS FOR 6 SERVINGS:
(depends on size of soup cup)

4 cups water

1 1" x 4" piece dried kombu seaweed

½ cup Kezuribushi (bonito flakes) or 1 tablespoon dashi no moto

4 tablespoons Aka miso

2 tablespoons sake

In a saucepan, bring water to a boil over medium heat. Place kombu in the water and remove from heat after 10 seconds. Add bonito flakes or dashi no moto.

Let stand 15 seconds; then strain through a wire-mesh strainer. If using dashi no moto, it is unnecessary to strain the soup. At this point you can add other ingredients like the head of the shrimp (from making butterflied shrimp), fresh fillet of fish or other seafood, or vegetables that have been lightly boiled. Cook for 2–3 minutes over medium heat (cooking time depends on type of ingredients). Remove from heat.

Pass the miso through the strainer into the soup, and stir to blend.

3

More Miso Soup Possibilities…

All ingredients that need to be boiled should be prepared before starting Step 2 above. Fresh ingredients should be added during Step 2.

1. Lightly steamed or boiled fish fillet (or leftover head & bones)
2. Fresh whole shrimp
3. Fresh flaked crab
4. Lightly boiled chicken, cut into bite-sized pieces
5. Cooked pork, sliced very thin
6. Cooked duck, sliced very thin
7. Poached egg—add an already-poached egg just before serving. (Lightly boiled or steamed thinly sliced potato, onion, carrot, and asparagus go well with the egg)
8. Tofu cut into small cubes
9. Wakame seaweed (fresh or reconstituted)
10. Nameko mushroom
11. Fresh or grilled wild mushrooms cut into bite-sized pieces
12. Boiled potato, peeled and sliced to size before boiling
13. Boiled sweet potato, peeled and sliced to size before boiling
14. Fresh onion, sliced
15. Fresh bean sprouts
16. Fresh carrot, sliced as desired
17. Fresh spinach (Japanese spinach should be boiled before adding)
18. Fresh eggplant cut to size as desired (fried eggplant is also great!)
19. Fresh snow peas, tips removed
20. Fresh asparagus spears, cut to include tips and tender part of stem only

GARNISHES:
1. Green onions (scallions), minced
2. Chilli powder

Mmm. Doesn't this look good! It's miso soup with a shrimp head and scallion garnish.

4

Suimono
Fish-Flavored Clear Soup

About Suimono...

It's suimono, not miso, which is actually the ultimate soup to serve with sushi. Unlike miso soup, which is an everyday soup for us, suimono has a noble image for the Japanese. Suimono is also like espresso coffee; it's not the kind of soup that tastes good after long cooking over a hot stove. But never fear—it's so easy and quick to prepare that you'll understand why we make or heat each portion just before serving.

If you use dashi no moto (instant fish soup powder), it's best to check the flavor before buying. Sardine flavor is not suitable for suimono. This delicate soup may also be made with any fresh fish you have on hand, instead of using soup powder and bonito flakes as seasonings. (See my list of variations on the next page.)

INGREDIENTS FOR 6–8 SERVINGS:
(depends on size of soup cup)

4 cups mineral water

½ cup sake

11" x 4" piece dried kombu seaweed

½ cup Kezuribushi (bonito flakes) or 1 tablespoon dashi no moto

2 teaspoons sea salt

A few drops of soy sauce

1 medium carrot, sliced and steamed or boiled

⅓ cup fresh spinach, stems removed, steamed or boiled

¼ cup daikon strips, lightly steamed or boiled

1 Place the water and sake in a medium saucepan. Bring to a boil and add the kombu. Remove with chopsticks after 10 seconds.

2 Add the bonito and strain out after 15 seconds. (Or add the dashi no moto.)

Variety of Ingredients for Suimono

All ingredients that need to be boiled should be prepared before starting Step 2 above. Fresh ingredients should be added during Step 2.

1. Lightly boiled fish fillet (or leftover head and bones)
2. Grilled fish fillet—flaked
3. Boiled peeled shrimp—boiled in dashi soup and peeled
4. Kamaboko (ready-made fish dumpling) sliced $1/8$" thick
5. Boiled chicken cut into bite-sized pieces
6. Lightly boiled chicken "meatball"—minced chicken with ginger and salt
7. Poached egg—add to the finished soup. Goes well with steamed carrot, spinach, asparagus, etc., or fresh snow peas
8. Tofu, cubed
9. Wakame seaweed, fresh or reconstituted
10. Fresh or grilled wild mushroom, cut into bite-sized pieces
11. Fresh radish, sliced as desired
12. Fresh carrot, sliced as desired
13. Fresh spinach (if using Japanese spinach, boil before using)
14. Fresh snow peas
15. Fresh green onion cut $1^1/2$"–$2^1/2$" long
16. Fresh asparagus tips (with tender part of stem only)

GARNISHES FOR READY PORTION OF SUIMONO:

Fresh green onion (scallions), minced
A few drops of yuzu orange or lime juice

Add the sea salt.
Add a few drops of soy sauce.

3

Add the boiled or steamed carrots, spinach, and radish.

4

Here's how it looks when it's done.

5

In this last chapter of the book, I'm feeling a little nostalgic, so I decided to close with these very special sushi, the kind you'll never find in sushi bars. These are the sushi that you'd probably find a Japanese mother or grandmother busy making out of all kinds of leftovers she has at home. The techniques are fun and the ingredients are flexible, so feel free to experiment, and explore your own creativity! I give examples of a few variations with each one, just for starters.

Kawarizushi

Ohinasama Chirashi
Salmon & Broiled Eel

"Chirashi" is simply sushi rice with topping, served in a sushi-oke (traditional sushi pot). "Ohinasama Hinamatsuri" means Girls' Day, and although this is not exactly the traditional sushi served on that holiday in Japan (a traditional one might be decorated with a cherry blossom that begins to appear at the same time in March), it's the one my daughter likes best!

INGREDIENTS FOR 1:

2 cups sushi rice

1 tablespoon sesame seeds, toasted in a dry frying pan

½ tablespoon chopped pickled ginger

1 rounded tablespoon flaked grilled salmon

1 rounded tablespoon chopped Unagi Kabayaki (see recipe p. 61)

1 teaspoon sakura denbu (sweet cod powder)

½ Seasoned Shitake Mushroom (see recipe p. 76) sliced thin (⅛")

1 asparagus tip, steamed or boiled and sliced 1½" long

1 teaspoon cooked sweet corn

Place the ingredients on a work surface.

1

Add the sesame seeds and ginger to the rice.

2

3 Use your fingers to mix the ingredients together.

4 Transfer the rice mixture to a sushi-oke or flat-bottomed ceramic bowl.

5 Add remaining ingredients and mix lightly.

Youfuu Oshizushi (Western-Style Pressed Sushi)
Salmon

Youfuu means "western," since as I mentioned before, salmon is not typically used for sushi or sashimi in Japan (although we do like it grilled or fried). This one is made with an oshizushi press, easily available at Japanese or Asian markets. Once you become crafty at sushi, you'll want to have your own press to play with.

INGREDIENTS FOR 6 PIECES, SERVES 2:

6 slices salmon fillet (½ oz. 2" long, 1½" wide, ⅛" thick)

6–8 tablespoons sushi rice

2 lemons, cut in half and sliced

fresh dill sprigs for garnish

1 Dip the entire frame of the oshizushi press in water and lightly dry with a paper towel. (This helps to make removal of ingredients easier.) Remove the cover from the press, and place the salmon fillets inside, with edges overlapping.

2 Place the rice over the salmon in an even layer.

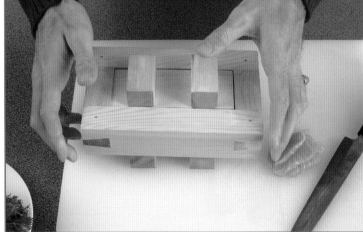

3 Replace the cover and press down lightly.

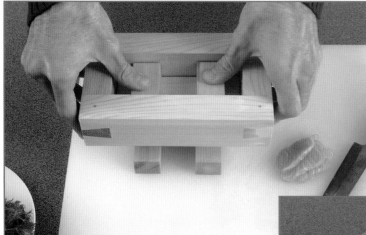

Use your thumbs to hold down the cover while you grasp the edges of the outer frame and remove it.

4

Turn over and remove the frame.

5

Slice the sushi in half and then slice each half into three pieces. Arrange on a serving plate with lemon slices in between. Garnish with dill. Serve with wasabi and ginger.

6

Sushi Cake
Chicken & Cashew Nut Teriyaki

My special sushi cake is made using something borrowed from western kitchens—a 2½" stainless steel pastry ring usually used for making perfectly round pancakes, eggs, or pastry. This recipe is great for everyone—especially those who prefer an alternative to fish—though you can use raw fish or any other topping if desired.

We make this sushi directly on the serving plate—once it's there you won't want to disturb it!

INGREDIENTS FOR EACH SERVING:

1 butterhead lettuce leaf
6 tablespoons sushi rice

INGREDIENTS FOR CHICKEN CASHEW TERIYAKI:

1 tablespoon chicken thigh meat, cut into ¼" chunks
1 tablespoon chopped cashew nuts
2 tablespoons teriyaki sauce
Chives for garnish

Before you begin to make the sushi, you need to prepare the filling: Grease a small frying pan with a little corn oil and gently stir-fry the chicken. Add the cashew nuts and continue to stir-fry 30 seconds. Pour in the teriyaki sauce, and cook over medium-low heat until the chicken is glazed and the sauce is reduced by half. May be served warm or cold.

1 Place a whole lettuce leaf on a serving platter. Wash the ring in cold water and dry with a paper towel. Place over the leaf.

2 Fill the ring with half the rice, pressing down lightly.

3 Spoon a layer of the prepared filling over the rice.

Make another layer of rice on top.

4

Use your thumbs to hold down the rice, while gently removing the ring with your fingers.

5

Place another spoonful of the chicken mixture on top.

6

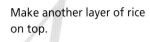

Garnish with the chives and serve.

7

Temarizushi
Tuna, Salmon & Avocado

"Te" means hand and "Mari" means ball. The name actually derives from the Samurai era, when the daughters of the wealthy samurais were given beautifully colored and designed (hand) balls, made of silk or other expensive materials, to play with. These are typical sushi that a Japanese mom would make at home—and kids (and friends) love to make them too!

INGREDIENTS FOR 3 PIECES:
3 rice balls, each made with:
1½ tablespoons sushi rice
1½" x 1½" x ⅛" thick slice of tuna
1½" x 1½" x ⅛" thick slice of salmon
1½" x 1½" x ⅛" thick slice of avocado
Minced chives
Salmon roe
Toasted black sesame seeds
1 teaspoon teriyaki sauce

1

Moisten hands with water-vinegar mixture and form 3 rice balls.

 Cut an 8" square of plastic wrap. Put one of the fillets in the middle. Place a rice ball on top of the fish fillet.

Bring up the corners of the plastic wrap to enclose the bundle.

Twist the edges tightly.

Repeat with the avocado, the other fillet and the remaining rice. Garnish the salmon with salmon roe, garnish the tuna with minced chives, and garnish the avocado with teriyaki sauce and black sesame seeds.

Saladmaki
Jumbo Shrimp & Lettuce

Japanese kids love mayonnaise (just like their American counterparts), so many a mother will use leftover jumbo shrimp, crab, fish dumplings, grilled chicken, or even smoked meats to make this sushi.

INGREDIENTS FOR I ROLL (6 PIECES):

1 sheet Nori

10–12 tablespoons sushi rice

3 boiled shrimps

Butterhead lettuce leaves

1 tablespoon Japanese or regular mayonnaise

Place the nori on a sushi mat. Moisten hands with water-vinegar mixture and flatten the rice on top, leaving 1" from the bottom and sides.

Cut the lettuce leaf in half and place on the rice. Put the shrimp and a squeeze of mayonnaise inside. Close the lettuce over the filling.

Now place your thumbs under the bottom of the sushi mat, and use the remaining fingers to hold the filling in place.

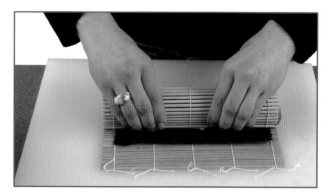

Bring the mat up to cover the filling, leaving 1" from the top edge of the nori. Enclose the roll and press firmly to tighten.

sushi for wimps

122

Raise the cover and bring forward slightly. Now close again over the entire roll firmly and remove the cover.

Slice the roll into 6 pieces. (Or slice the roll in half, and then each half into 3 pieces.)

Arrange on a serving platter with wasabi and ginger.

Index

Credits
Our Sushi Mavens

MICHAEL KINSBRUNER
Michael is a film student and producer of documentary films, with a passion for Akira Kurosawa and Japanese food. Although he kept trying to direct the photographer, and occasionally yelled "cut" at inappropriate times, Mike had just the angle on sushi that we needed. He particularly enjoyed the Arranged Sashimi "for its artistic qualities and clear-cut flavors." That's Mike!

RACHEL LITTLE
A gifted graphic designer, Rachel had always claimed that she was better with a palette knife than a sashimi bouchou, but she proved herself wrong. By the last session, she was even designing her own creations! She particularly enjoys saimaki rolls, citing their interplay of colors.

INGA GREVTOZ
Our exotic Scandinavian Inga, a yoga instructor who contemplated several days before deciding to join us in the studio, found sushi a totally new level of consciousness. Although particularly drawn to Norwegian Temaki, she was seen savoring more than a few vegetarian makis between asanas.

ADAM WEISSMAN

Adam's secret desire was to be a samurai or a surgeon, so he decided to study medicine, and make a practice out of sushi at the same time. A natural with a knife, Adam was especially eager to learn how to fillet a whole fish, or "dissect it," as he referred to it. Now we know he has patience. Already a sushi maven when he came to us, Adam claims he has a special yen for Takosumiso (chopped octopus) sashimi and Unagi (eel) nigiri.

SAL WEISSMAN

A medical student along with her brother Adam, Sal was our Madame Curie when it came to mixing and measuring. Although she had often enjoyed her brother's sushi, she had never actually observed his operations till our photo shoot, when she also got a hand at the knife. Sal loves temaki hand rolls, and Alaskan is her favorite.

LEA PENN

Lea was first introduced to sushi by Oscar, Aya's formerly "sushi wimp" friend. From there it was love at first bite. A theater student in New York (and sporting a set of very dramatic blonde curls), Lea quickly took center stage at our photo shoot, acting the role with conviction, and proving a natural born talent. Her favorites? Sushi Cake with Chicken & Cashew Nut Teriyaki ("enticing") and anything made with salmon.

NED IVORY

A drama student living in New York, Ned never knew a nigiri from a maki till he joined us in the studio. Although he frequently kept us in suspense, Ned turned in a serious performance as a sushi maven to rave reviews. His favorite: Kawa Suzuki Arai —which he claims was a chilling experience!